THE
WEALTH
OF
CITIES

THE
WEALTH
OF
CITIES

*Revitalizing the Centers
of American Life*

JOHN O. NORQUIST

Addison-Wesley
Reading, Massachusetts

Many of the designations used by manufacturers and sellers to distinguish their products are claimed as trademarks. Where those designations appear in this book and Addison-Wesley was aware of a trademark claim, the designations have been printed in initial capital letters.

Library of Congress Cataloging-in-Publication Data

Norquist, John O.
    The wealth of cities : revitalizing the centers of American life /
John O. Norquist.
        p.   cm.
    Includes bibliographical references (p.) and index.
    ISBN 0-201-44213-2
    1. Cities and towns—United States.   2. Urban policy—United
States.   3. Urban renewal—United States.   I. Title.
    HT123.N655   1998
    307.76'0973—dc21   97-32845
                                                                                              CIP

Addison-Wesley is an imprint of Addison Wesley Longman, Inc.

Jacket design by Suzanne Heiser
Text design by Diane Levy
Set in 10-point Stone Serif by Carlisle Communications

1 2 3 4 5 6 7 8 9-MA-0201009998
First printing, April 1998

Addison-Wesley books are available at special discounts for bulk purchases in the U.S. by corporations, institutions, and other organizations. For more information, please contact the Corporate, Government, and Special Sales Department at Addison Wesley Longman, Inc., One Jacob Way, Reading, MA 01867, or call 1-800-238-9682.

Find us on the World Wide Web at
http://www.aw.com/gb/

Contents

Introduction

We must restore to the city the maternal, life-nurturing functions, the autonomous activities, the symbiotic associations that have long been neglected or suppressed. For the city should be an organ of life; and the best economy of cities is the care and culture of human beings.
—Lewis Mumford

IN 1968 the *Kerner Report* was issued by an advisory commission appointed by President Lyndon Johnson. The commission's role was to attempt to understand the causes of the rioting that had occurred in several large U.S. cities in 1967 and to suggest policy changes to prevent future rioting. Among the suggested changes was a call for increased federal involvement in housing, transportation, and welfare. What the report did not acknowledge was that the federal government had already been involved in these areas, and to a great extent that involvement had helped create the negative conditions deplored by the commission.

For the past fifty years the suburban edges of U.S. cities have been encouraged to prosper, while the centers have been allowed to emulsify. First came segregated suburban housing, developed with federal subsidies. Then came subsidized highways to service the commuter communities; then retail shopping malls; and eventually, the workplace itself moved to the suburbs, in the form of office parks. In Detroit, Los Angeles, and to varying degrees all U.S. cities, the disassembled ingredients of the city sprawled across the suburban landscape, while large central cities have done little more than draw attention to their own pathologies by crying out for help from a federal government encrusted in a $5 trillion debt.

IN THIS BOOK, I try to change the discussion from how to help our dying cities to how our still-vital cities add lasting value to the United States and can, if allowed, add even more value, in spite of the damage done them. I begin with a brief discussion of how cities have been deeply harmed by federal and state policies, including some policies intended to help them. Cities have too often been willing victims in this process, lining up like beggars at the trough of federal largesse.

I outline the natural advantages that could allow cities to lead an economic and cultural renaissance in the twenty-first century. Their physical properties—scale, proximity, and diversity—are their chief advantage. The benefits that accrue where large numbers of diverse people live and work closely together include the most efficient results in transportation, labor exchange, consumption, capital allocation, culture, and education.

A second advantage of cities lies in their origins and their organic nature. Unlike counties, states, and nations, most cities formed as marketplaces. With a few exceptions, such as Washington, D.C., cities were created by human interaction and market forces, not by government, and they would exist regardless of the form of government.

I argue that cities can thrive, naturally and organically, if certain steps are taken. Most important are steps that cities can take themselves, particularly in budgeting, management, public safety, and design. Cities must become the safest, healthiest, most affordable, and most beautiful places they can possibly be. New York, Philadelphia, Chicago, Portland, Oregon, Indianapolis, and Milwaukee, among other cities, are heading in this direction. As cities reduce crime and taxes, the physical appeal of the urban form becomes apparent and attractive to potential residents and businesses.

Introduction

I also discuss state and federal policies that are damaging to cities and how they must be changed if the United States is to avoid becoming a sprawling collection of faceless places, neither urban nor rural, and with no lasting value.

Welfare must be replaced with work, not workfare. School choice must expand from experiment to norm. The federal government must step out of the housing business and allow the market to recreate affordable housing that was once so broadly available. U.S. international trade policy should purge special-interest influence and allow U.S. merchants and manufacturers to trade freely. Environmental regulations should recognize the inherent benefits of cities, follow market principles to the extent possible, and be strictly enforced. Urban superhighways should be relegated to the scrap heap of history, and defederalization of our surface transportation system should be considered, allowing for major local and regional investments in transit, pedestrian, and bicycle routes integrated with the time-tested, traditional street grid. Most of these changes, the same changes that can make our cities rich again for the most part, demand less rather than more from state and federal governments.

THE WEALTH OF CITIES is for taxpayers, mayors, bureaucrats, scholars, investors, developers, and home owners. It is meant to speak for those who love cities but have forgotten why, and it seeks to persuade those who have never loved cities that they are worthy, if not of love, at least of respect, and to realize that cities add value to the nation. This book is for people who hope for a richer and more civilized United States of America.

Acknowledgments

I THANK Mitch Metz for research and crucial counsel. William Patrick, formerly of Addison Wesley Longman, provided key advice and what almost every first-time author needs: strict deadlines. My editor, Nick Philipson, and his assistant, Eric Rickstad, helped me immensely. Much thanks to my book agent, Glen Hartley, for believing in the value of my ideas.

You Can't Build a City on Pity

WHEN THE RODNEY KING verdict was announced in 1992, a riot erupted in south central Los Angeles. The rioters killed fifty people, torched over six hundred structures, and caused a billion dollars of property damage. The riot dominated newspaper headlines. CNN provided twenty-four-hour television coverage, featuring live shots from a corner where rampaging youths pulled a man from his truck and beat him to within an inch of his life. For a few days our national consciousness focused on this riot, on this troubled neighborhood, and on the frightened city of Los Angeles. Jack Kemp, secretary of housing and urban development, visited the scene. Bill Clinton, front-runner for the Democratic nomination for president, visited too.

President George Bush appointed Peter Ueberoth, former baseball commissioner and director of the 1984 Olympics in Los Angeles, czar of the south Los Angeles recovery effort, and Bush himself stopped in L.A. to demonstrate his concern.

In reaction to the riot and the ensuing press coverage, the United States Conference of Mayors (USCM) Advisory Board held a meeting three thousand miles away at its Washington, D.C., headquarters, located a convenient few blocks from the White House. The topic: how to capitalize on the riot and convince the federal government to establish an urban agenda. The mayors' organization seemed to be saying that the riot was not the action of lawless thugs willing to trash their own community, but, rather, a demonstration of the need for

1

a federal urban policy. It was as though USCM leadership viewed the rioters as a sort of violent cadre of lobbyists for urban issues.

As mayor of Milwaukee and a member of the board, I went to this meeting, this think session. The problem was that no one seemed to be thinking. We were wishing. USCM staff encouraged the mayors to wish out loud "what we should ask for" now that George Bush and others were suddenly paying attention to cities. Excitement ran through the room. For the mayors it was like a chance to sit on Santa Claus's lap and ask for federal presents.

Some mayors wanted to increase federal block grants. Mayor Marion Barry of Washington, D.C., thought it was time to call for the return of federal revenue sharing, citing legislation introduced by Congressman John Conyers of Detroit. Others agreed that we should ask for revenue sharing, but suggested calling it by a different name. They felt that since most members of Congress viewed revenue sharing as a budget buster, calling it something else might make it more acceptable.

My turn came. I agreed that we had the federal government's attention, but I wasn't happy with how we got it. And I suspected it wouldn't last long. As soon as CNN stopped covering the riot, as soon as the major candidates stopped scheduling appearances to emote their concern, only two groups of people would remember what had happened in any meaningful way.

The first group would comprise the people in the neighborhood who had lived through a nightmare and would pay its price for a long time to come. The other group would consist of bankers, insurance companies, and investors from around the world who would be reluctant to put their money where it seemed likely to burn. Not only would these people long remember to keep their money out of south central Los Angeles, but, to the extent that they looked at the riot as a problem shared by all large U.S. cities—which is precisely how we mayors were asking everyone to view it—they would withhold money from all our cities.

In seeking federal aid we were sending a repulsive message to private capital markets. Imagine the CEO of a private corporation

You Can't Build a City on Pity

telling the corporation's customers and stockholders that the corporation was out of money and that if it didn't get more money soon it would burn. Imagine how customers would react: they'd look for new suppliers. Imagine how stockholders would react: they'd sell their stock. Yet cities were telling their investors and stockholders just that.

Four years later, an article by Elizabeth Gleck in *Time* magazine documented the lack of reinvestment in south central Los Angeles and the frustrations of a man named Terrence Payne. Payne had been unable to finance and rebuild his grocery store and rental apartments that were destroyed in the riot. Special programs for riot victims hadn't been effective. Gleck reported, "Payne has jumped through more hoops than a circus tiger and still has not managed to cobble together the financing to rebuild." A *Wall Street Journal* story reinforced the message. "Some of the promised funding didn't materialize," it read. "In addition, many businesspeople were simply leery of setting up in the area after the violence."

In 1992 south central Los Angeles was in the limelight as an object of pity. If good intentions were worth money, it would now be the wealthiest spot in the United States. It's not. For south central Los Angeles, the pity turned to neglect and contempt.

TWO YEARS EARLIER, in the fall of 1990, New York City mayor David Dinkins had organized a meeting for the mayors of the fifty largest cities in the United States, from the metropolis of New York to the edge city of Arlington, Texas. The Berlin Wall had fallen the year before, and with the diminished Soviet threat came widespread hope that deep cuts in U.S. military spending could help fund domestic needs. Dinkins wanted to discuss "the peace dividend and how to plan for it and how to get it." Leading up to the meeting, Boston mayor Raymond Flynn had called U.S. cities "western versions of Beirut." Meanwhile, press analysts wrote off mayors as whiners, saying, "Instead of offering political advantages to the federal administrations . . . they can only offer the nagging problems of the large urban centers."

As a member of the USCM Advisory Board, I had attended many board meetings where valuable time was soaked up by staff reports about the latest congressional appropriation opportunities for cities. These meetings were run almost as if USCM director Tom Cochrane and his staff wanted to keep the mayors from talking to each other. Perhaps they believed that if the mayors conversed, they might discover how stale and ineffective the organization had become. In contrast, Dinkins hosted a turbulent and productive session. In an unprecedented move, rather than have the meeting run by staff, Dinkins had the insight to allow mayors and only mayors to speak to each other.

At the meeting I presented a paper attacking as absurd and counterproductive the USCM strategy of begging the federal government for money. I argued that valuable cities such as New York, Chicago, San Francisco, Boston, Seattle, and Milwaukee should not be on their knees seeking alms from a federal government both encrusted in debt and openly hostile to cities. My paper caused a stir and served as a focal point for further discussion.

My message was simple, but for the USCM it was revolutionary: you can't build a city on fear, and you can't build a city on pity. Appealing to these emotions might generate a few dollars at first, but fear soon turns to hatred and pity to contempt. No one, particularly no one with money—whether the federal government or private investors—likes to be around a loser.

Mayors must rid themselves of the self-pity that focuses on urban pathology and ignores the advantages and virtues of cities thus undermining the ability of cities to compete in the marketplace. You *can* build a city on its natural advantages: its efficient proximity and density, its processes and markets, and its extraordinary capacity to promote the success of its citizens. I called for a new strategy to highlight and reinforce these urban advantages.

You Can't Build a City on Pity

Although cities are governed, the fundamental nature of a city is not that of a unit of government. Remove the idea of municipal government and Denver or Memphis, for instance, would still function as a city, although its boundaries would be less distinct. The same cannot be said of individual states, nations, and empires. Cities result from trade, from the interaction of people through markets, not from the edicts of emperors or kings or the machinations of legislators or presidents.

Cities are extraordinarily complex organisms, but their complexity derives from a simple formula. Cities form as people gather together. Large numbers of people living close together communicate, work, trade, sell, buy, and specialize easily and thus to a greater degree than do people who live far apart from one another.

The efficient proximity of people in cities and the consequent ease of interaction unleash processes that build civilization. Cities foster specialization of labor and concentration of capital. Specialized labor results in leisure time, which can be devoted to creating art, music, religion, and culture; concentrated capital, which essentially *is* wealth, fosters greater productivity, as cities allocate resources toward building bridges, sewer systems, and transportation networks, usually through government, and producing goods and services through markets.

Mayors and urban dwellers—all of us—need to renew our appreciation of cities and to remember the positive qualities of cities that over the course of history have created the world's great civilizations. We need to stop viewing cities as problems and government as the only cure. We need to work to put into place new polices that strengthen the natural ability of cities to foster wealth and culture and to build civilization.

Chasing Eden

Poet Carl Sandburg wrote "Chicago," his powerful anthem to urban life, in 1916, only six years after he served as secretary to Milwaukee mayor Emil Seidel, the first Socialist mayor in the United States. The poem describes the city of Chicago as vibrant and brimming with life.

During the first third of the twentieth century cities were chasing an American Eden. While pounding out the pulse of the nation, cities held the hearts of the people in their big, calloused hands. Sandburg believed they had license to laugh even from beneath the "terrible burden of destiny."

In many ways, my own city of Milwaukee shared with Chicago the surging vitality of early-twentieth-century urban life. We also shared the name for a major street, Grand Avenue. *Grand* is a good word to describe Milwaukee in 1910, when Carl Sandburg worked there. Civic-minded Milwaukeeans threw their support behind an art museum, exposition building, public museum, public library, skating rinks, public bath, and zoo. The zoo, founded nineteen years earlier with seven deer donated by the Auer and Pabst families, had just welcomed Countess Heinie, its first elephant. Grand Avenue, often simply called the Avenue, was the city's main commercial thoroughfare, packed with merchants and shoppers from all over the world. The Avenue dominated the commerce not only of Milwaukee, but of the state of Wisconsin.

By 1910, automobiles, considered toys for the wealthy only a few years earlier, were vying for space on the Avenue with pedestrians, bicyclists, carriages, and streetcars. Milwaukee Electric Railway owned 140 miles of trolley tracks. It also served over more than thirteen thousand electric customers. It was a good idea to live near a trolley route if you wanted electric and telephone service.

Pabst Brewery had just surpassed the Joseph Schlitz Brewing Company a few doors down to become the largest brewer in the United States. Much of its product was consumed locally. "Every weekday at 6:30 A.M. drivers and their teams lined up in the Pabst Brewery yards to carry lager to a thirsty city," observed local historian Robert Wells. Wealthy families, finding themselves short of beer, could order direct from the brewery and see the product deliv-

You Can't Build a City on Pity

ered in a handsome carriage by uniformed attendants. In 1910, August Uihlein, the major shareholder in Schlitz, was the wealthiest person in Milwaukee.

That summer Ole Evinrude was in the process of selling twenty-five outside-the-stern engines to boat-owning lakeside dwellers. He had gotten the idea five years earlier when on a picnic with his fiancée; she wanted an ice cream cone and he had to row across a local lake to get it. Evinrude and Milwaukee soon became synonymous with the outboard motor.

In the Merrill Park neighborhood, the Milwaukee Road and St. Rose's Church dominated the lives of the Irish immigrants who lived there. The Milwaukee Road provided jobs to over five thousand workers, and St. Rose's provided just about everything else. Pubs filled in the gaps.

On the near north side, young Goldie Mabovitch was attending Fourth Street School. Nine years later, as Mrs. Goldie Myerson, she quit her job at the library to emigrate to Palestine. She became better known later as Golda Meir, prime minister of Israel.

In 1910, grand Milwaukee, the twelfth largest city in the United States, was also a city in transition. That year's election of Socialist mayor Emil Seidel ushered in an era of gravity and responsibility that had been absent during the previous five terms of mayor and rapscallion David "All-the-Time-Rosy" Rose. Seidel shut down the River Street red-light district and padlocked houses presided over by madams Kitty Williams and her rival Jeanette Hampton. The tourist trade, particularly from Chicago, plummeted. Some heartier fun seekers still found adventure on Jones Island, located in the Milwaukee harbor and populated by about two thousand Polish fishermen known as Kasubes. Local lore had it that "all the men do there is fish, drink, and fight, and in winter they don't fish."

Milwaukee's economy was shifting gears as well, from grain shipping, trade, and nightlife to manufacturing. The great immigration of the mid- and late 1800s was coming to a close. Three-quarters of all Milwaukee citizens were either born abroad or had at least one parent of foreign ancestry. Among large cities, Milwaukee was second only to New York in percentage of foreign-born residents. Fortunately for early-twentieth-century Milwaukee, it had caught the immigration wave of 1848. Many of these midcentury arrivals were not typical immigrants—farmers, serfs, and unskilled laborers escaping poverty in the Old World and arriving to build the agrarian backbone of their new country. Rather, Milwaukee's midcentury influx included highly educated and skilled immigrants, many of whom came to the United States to escape political persecution. Fifty years later, their education and skills paid dividends as Milwaukee shifted to a manufacturing economy. With its high concentration of machinists, tool and die makers, and industrial designers, Milwaukee became known as the "Toolbox of the World."

Grand Milwaukee's prosperity only increased during the next two decades. From 1916 to 1924, its manufacturing output nearly tripled. The port's lake tonnage surpassed that of Chicago. The city population grew by 100,000, from about 420,000 to about 520,000 residents. Crime remained virtually unknown, with a murder rate about 10 percent that of other large U.S. cities. Financial analysts considered Milwaukee's credit among the best of any U.S. city. In his 1928 inaugural speech, Mayor Dan Hoan noted that Milwaukee was the second most densely populated city in the United States, next to New York City.

The *gemütlichkeit* of the German Athens was by no means perfect. Order and personal responsibility coexisted with legal prostitution and gambling parlors. There was rank discrimination against African Americans and class warfare between the barons of industry and a socialist trade-union movement. Working conditions were often dangerous. Poor public health was a major concern. But in Milwaukee, as in most cities, people felt that things were getting better. Cities proudly chased an American vision of Eden, sometimes stumbling in that chase, but believing in the inevitability of a better life for all.

Then the Great Depression struck, and cities were suddenly in deep trouble.

Original Sin

By 1933 many cities were struggling with 50 percent unemployment. As starvation, violence, and despair threatened urban centers, they were tempted to seek federal help. The temptation was so great that the mayors of the nation's largest cities hired a lobbyist and formed an association, the United States Conference of Mayors (USCM). Led by Milwaukee mayor Dan Hoan, Boston mayor James Michael Curley, Detroit mayor Frank Murphy, and New York mayor Jimmy Walker, the USCM approached Capitol Hill, tin cups in hand.

Mayor Hoan described the detailed analysis that went into the USCM's decision to ask for money:

> *"[S]omeone said, 'Well gentlemen, we've got to get down to business. What are we going to do about this depression?' There wasn't a soul in the room who had an idea. They were just as dumb as they were in Washington. It was as if somebody kicked them in the stomach, and they couldn't get their breath. They didn't know what the hell it was all about."*
>
> *Hoan recalled that he finally broke the silence by saying, "Gentlemen, if nobody else has got a motion, I'll make one. . . . I move that we go to Washington and that we ask them to set up five billion dollars for public work."*

Even in their desperation and "dumbness," as Hoan termed it, the mayors knew enough to ask only for temporary jobs programs; they did not ask for direct federal subsidization of municipal budgets.

Some mayors opposed federal help entirely. Earlier, Hoan had sent letters to the mayors of the hundred largest cities in the United States asking for their thoughts on a federal relief program "commensurate with what we have done in the past for the starving peoples of Europe." Only twenty-two responded, five of them negatively. Trenton's mayor, Frederick W. Donnelly, thought a federal program would be "an invasion of community rights."

But at the subsequent USCM meeting the mayors of Denver, Richmond, Virginia, and Syracuse, New York, were the only dissenters. They felt that cities could continue carrying on alone. They warned the other mayors not to "further complicate our national crisis by another demand on federal resources that do not exist." They foresaw too much federal intervention in city matters. According to Mark I. Gelfand in *A Nation of Cities*, "The Democratic mayor of Richmond told the meeting that if municipalities would simply learn to live within their incomes, all their problems would disappear."

The USCM soon got what it asked for. And more, as we shall see. On the heels of temporary help, such as the well-conceived jobs programs, came more permanent—and intrusive—help from the federal government.

Detroit's Murphy and Milwaukee's Hoan were the USCM's principal organizers. Boston's James Michael Curley was its point man, its mouthpiece of relentless importunity. Not only was Curley among those who invented the concept of federal help for cities, but he was so obsessed with the idea that he occasionally *imagined* federal help for Boston.

"Curley first descended on Washington on February 1, 1935, asking for relief assistance totaling $160 million," wrote Jack Beatty in *The Rascal King*. "The relief authorities . . . ignored him. A few weeks later he claimed he had federal backing for the construction of a $40 million sewer system."

Once the highest achievement of U.S. culture, cities began to be defined as the problem, even by themselves. In 1932, Paul Betters, the executive director of the American Municipal Association, wrote to Detroit mayor Murphy, "The crying need in America today is for the public to realize that essentially our national problems are *municipal* or urban problems, and the mayors could materially focus public attention on this fact."

Chicago mayor Anton Cermak added to this perception by issuing threats to get money. In a technique mimicking that of his city's most infamous depression-era residents, Cermak told Congress that violence would erupt in the streets of Chicago if the federal government didn't step in. "It would be cheaper for Congress to provide a loan of $152 million to the City of Chicago, than to pay for the services of federal troops at a future date," he said.

When World War II started, the depression ended quietly and virtually everyone had work. The U.S. government used all its money and borrowing capacity to wage war. Federal money for cities dried up, but the memory of those funds lingered. The conditions that drew Hoan and Murphy to Washington, D.C., no longer existed, but the mayors, having tasted federal relief, wanted more. They were bolder and better organized. A permanent financial relationship with Washington had become the purpose of the USCM.

The Flood

After the war, federal transfer payments to cities gradually increased, in part to replace the lost economic stimulus of World War II. The aid was targeted for public housing and urban renewal. In 1949, Title I of the housing act committed $500 million in aid over five years and Congress added a few hundred million more each year in 1954, 1957, and 1959. Then came the roads: $15 billion to begin implementation of the 1956 Interstate Highway Act.

Referring to the start-up of the interstate highway system, U.S. Senator Daniel Patrick Moynihan remarked, "It was possible to see that these roads were too big for our cities and that they were going to smash them to pieces. . . . You could see it happening but you couldn't get anyone to hear you."

The 1950s were a prosperous time. After a short, deep recession at the end of the war, the economy boomed. Yet Presidents Dwight D. Eisenhower and John F. Kennedy lacked the will to end transfer payments to cities, and Presidents Lyndon Johnson and Richard Nixon didn't want to. The 1960s ushered in the Great Society, and a steady rain of federal money started falling on cities. The riots of 1965 and 1968 confirmed Cermak's warning; violence did erupt in the streets of Chicago, and elsewhere. The Kerner Commission report made it to the *New York Times* best-seller list with its call for action and warning of "a nation divided" by race and income. Between 1960 and 1974, federal grants to state and local governments rose from $7 billion to nearly $45 billion. It was the perfect environment for mayors to launch their "crusade for resources."

Leading that crusade was Henry Maier, mayor of Milwaukee. The resource he sought from 1960 to 1988 was federal aid, and his skill in mobilizing an urban coalition to support the crusade became legendary. In his first speech as mayor, his 1960 inaugural address, over one-third of the text was devoted to asking other units of government for help. Maier managed not to propose a single city-funded program or solution. When reelected in 1972, he was also serving as president of the USCM, and he pledged to Milwaukeeans to "continue to exert our efforts for a city sharing in the richest revenue source in the nation, the federal income tax." Another twelve years passed, and his politically successful formula had not changed. Maier's 1984 inaugural address insisted, "There is a challenge to win Milwaukee's fair share of resources from Madison and Washington— and to work with our sister cities to bring about an administration in Washington that revives a national urban policy."

Maier parlayed his relentless pursuit of state and federal dollars into a national leadership role, alongside Richard Daley and others. His goals were not unique among his colleagues; he was just better at achieving them.

You Can't Build a City on Pity

In 1972 the mayors hit the jackpot. President Richard Nixon started giving cities cash, lots of cash, in the form of no-strings-attached federal revenue sharing. What had been a steady rain from Washington for the perpetually parched cities turned into a deluge of unrestricted federal aid. It rained day and night for thirteen years. From 1974 through 1986, Milwaukee alone received more than $160 million in revenue sharing.

Former Milwaukee legislative coordinator Dick Heaps tells this story about Milwaukee's first federal revenue-sharing check:

Naturally, we were all patting each other on the back. The checks were going to come quarterly, but the first one, for some accounting reason in Washington, was delayed and covered the first five quarters of the program. It was a big check: $15 million.

Maier couldn't wait to get his dream come true and would call our Congressmen every day to try to speed things up. Finally, we heard that the check was cut but, again for some reason known only to Washington, would not be mailed for two or three days. This was before electronic transfer.

So I asked the mayor if the city would spring for a plane ticket to D.C.—I'd go pick up the check in person.

"What?" he said, "If the press got hold of that, I'd be crucified!"

"Mayor," I replied, "Do you have any idea how much interest $15 million earns in four or five days?" And I told him. His jaw dropped.

Well, I didn't get the trip to D.C., but Maier did manage to find a way to earn interest on our money in D.C. until the check was mailed to the city.

Eventually, Jimmy Carter capped revenue-sharing payments. Later, Ronald Reagan cut them back and finally, with the quiet help of the Democratic Congress, killed the program entirely, thus ending the crusade for resources. Well, almost. The Community Development Block Grants that Nixon started in 1974, for example, remain in place. Now the principal source of federal aid to cities, they provide about $4.5 billion in flexible money nationwide. The most recent aid came from President Bill Clinton through the 1995 Crime Bill. Clinton told cities to add police officers, and he partially paid for them.

The effect of this residue of federal aid is not so much to build cities, but to keep mayors wandering in the wilderness, waiting for bread to fall from on high. Perhaps as mayors we hope to return to Eden, to a time of optimism, when urban success led the nation to prosperity.

Living Cities and Urban Doomsayers

We think of cities, states, nations, and empires as different sizes of the same things, like circles within circles. Cities occupy a small area and help make up a state. Several states form a nation. From time to time diverse nations are forged into an empire.

This hierarchical worldview overlooks the distinction between cities and every other form of political or geographic organization. Cities form naturally. Cities are organic. Whereas armies create empires, politicians found nations, members of Congress create states, and legislators draw county boundaries, it is usually commerce that creates and sustains cities.

Cities grow, trade, produce, erect buildings, evolve neighborhoods, send out thoroughfares, spin off factories and stores and churches and theaters and universities—with or without higher forms of government. They may be helped or damaged by government, but they are not the creatures of government. And as empires and nations come and go, some even in this decade, cities, with few exceptions, endure.

I have read books and articles by George Gilder, Joel Garreau, David Rusk, and other urban doomsayers who discuss the demise of U.S. cities. So many have predicted the end of our cities that I sometimes wonder if I'm dreaming as I walk around Milwaukee—or Chicago, Seattle, Portland, San Francisco, New Orleans, Cleveland, Charleston, Baltimore, Philadelphia, Boston, or New York—and see so many people going to work, making and selling products and services, meeting each other's needs, and enjoying life. If our cities lie on their deathbeds, they're sure having fun in their final moments.

Most urban doomsayers fall into one of two camps. The first camp claims that our cities are dead or dying; "I think we are headed for the death of cities," says futurist George Gilder. The members of this group differ as to whether the demise of cities is a uniquely American event or a worldwide phenomenon. They also disagree on the cause of the demise. Some, like Gilder, say technology; others say racism; still others blame failures of government in the areas of housing integration and land-use planning. Whatever the cause of death, this group of urban undertakers agree that there's no point trying to revive cities. The best we can do is arrange for a decent funeral, that is, help people leave.

The members of the second group are more like medical technicians than true urban undertakers. They subscribe to the view that our cities are *almost* dead and can only be revived with outside intervention, such as massive amounts of federal aid. This camp doesn't offer a different diagnosis, simply a different prognosis. Their cure, however, requires either huge infusions of federal money—a return to revenue sharing, an increase in block grants, expanded enterprise zones, big new tax credits—or politically impossible schemes to expand city boundaries through regional government or annexation. Whatever medicine they prescribe, the name of the treatment is often the same; to rescue our cities, these people say, we need a new, urban Marshall Plan.

I disagree with both camps. U.S. cities are not dead. They are not even dying. It is true that cities in the United States have been damaged. It is also true that they are in significant ways worse off than are their counterparts in Canada, Europe, and Asia. But they are far from terminal.

History shows that as nations and empires come and go, cities endure. The city of Damascus, for example, is four thousand years old. It has survived the Assyrian, Greek, Roman, and Ottoman empires and thrives even today under the modern state of Syria, one of the most oppressive regimes in the world. Damascus lives because it remains relevant and useful to commerce and culture. Killing a city requires burning it to the ground—usually several times—as with Troy or Carthage.

I also disagree with those urban doomsayers, including many big-city mayors, who say our cities can be rescued only through massive federal spending. Although to the extent that U.S. cities suffer economically, it is largely (though not entirely) the fault of the federal government, the solution is not an urban Marshall Plan.

We should try neither to bury nor to rescue cities. Instead, we need to unlock the potential of cities through a series of changes in federal transportation, welfare, housing, and budget policies that will result in less spending, a smaller, less intrusive federal government, the end of federal deficits, the rapid reduction of the federal debt, and the restoration of the wealth-generating ability of cities. In order to identify national and local policies that inhibit the wealth-producing potential of cities, we need a better understanding of how cities foster wealth in the first place.

The Advantage of Cities

Athens, Damascus, Tenochtitlán, and other ancient cities formed as people's occupations expanded beyond hunting, gathering, and farming for subsistence. Coming together at sites that offered reliable food sources, people formed loose, semipermanent villages to protect themselves from animals, robbers, and invaders. Their basic needs met, they began to specialize, first as laborers, homemakers, priests, soldiers, merchants, artisans, and educators.

In his *City in History,* Lewis Mumford posits that the village, although able to generate some marginal degree of wealth and leisure, was not sufficient to turn wealth and leisure into culture. Economic specialization and safety needed another ingredient: density. Only when loose villages became routinely defined by permanent walls did true cities emerge.

You Can't Build a City on Pity

Mumford calls this process implosion. "The many diverse elements of the community hitherto scattered . . . were mobilized and packed together under pressure behind the massive walls of the city. . . . The city was the container that brought about . . . implosion, and through its very form held together the new forces, intensified their internal reactions, and raised the whole level of achievement."

The Latin word *civitas* is the root for both city and civilization. Cities fostered civilization. Cities provided environments in which thousands—and later hundreds of thousands and eventually millions—of human beings could mingle together with their special knowledge and skills, resulting in the creation of markets and wealth. This phenomenon was not lost on London's Samuel Johnson in 1785 when he said, "Men, thinly scattered, make a go, but a bad go, without many things. . . . It is being concentrated which produces convenience."

People living and working together bring about the mix of communication, supply, demand, invention, creativity, and productivity needed to fuel enterprise and generate profit. And only if profit exists—whether it is the working person's small savings or the giant corporation's large surplus—are resources available to advance art, education, and culture.

Winston Churchill understood the value of profit to culture building. He defended it to Labour opponents in 1959, saying that some look at private enterprise as a predatory tiger to be shot, while others look at it as a cow they can milk. The truth, he said, is that private enterprise is a strong horse that pulls the cart along.

Of the many ways in which cities foster wealth, five stand out.

Transportation

Cities facilitate the conduct of commerce. They are destinations. In cities people and products are concentrated, making for nearly frictionless markets. With the help of modern technology and such modern strategies as futures trading, commerce involving trillions of dollars takes place every day in the markets of cities around the world.

Physical proximity is enhanced by the design of cities and the variety of urban transportation options. Cities support intricate grids of streets, alleys, and sidewalks that allow easy access of workers to jobs, suppliers to producers, customers to shops, firms to markets, diners to restaurants, worshipers to churches, moviegoers to theaters, and so forth, by foot, bike, car, bus, trolley, or train.

Urban transportation systems, unless disrupted by outside forces, greatly reduce the time and costs incurred in moving people and products around. By accelerating the pace and lowering the costs of both business and personal life, cities provide a setting that naturally generates wealth.

Labor Exchange

Cities expedite the exchange of labor. In cities, the basic ingredients of economic success—a large and diverse supply of labor and demand for it—are aided by a sophisticated system of getting workers into the right jobs fast. This system includes ways to signal the opportunity for work (word of mouth, newspaper advertising, temporary-placement agencies, specialized publications); methods of fitting together workers and jobs (job interviews, job testing, on-the-job training); techniques for changing the caliber of the labor supply (education and training); and means of changing the profiles of demand (altering wages or modifying benefits).

As a result, cities are the fastest and most efficient places for workers to get the jobs they really want and for businesses to find the employees they need to succeed. Cities quickly link enterprises with the muscle and brains they need to prosper.

Consumption

Cities ease the consumption of goods and services. In cities, consumers are close to an amazing variety and concentration of goods

You Can't Build a City on Pity

and services: everyday necessities, such as groceries, clothing, and hardware; leisure activities, such as dining, movies, and ball games; occasional purchases, including cars, refrigerators, and computers; and even rarer purchases, such as houses or works of art.

People can buy or rent virtually anything, usually from several vendors—sometimes a dozen or more, or even a thousand, depending on the product—in a city. Thus urban proximity also gives consumers access to aggressive competition among vendors. Competition improves the quality and lowers the cost of products for consumers and spurs merchants and manufacturers to become more productive. Urban proximity makes the national economy more efficient and more competitive internationally. By allowing consumers to get more for their money and by rewarding productivity of vendors, urban marketplaces generate resources that can be spent on further consumption and investment.

Capital Allocation

Cities make it easy to allocate capital well. Because people in cities work close to each other, they know what business others are engaged in, whether it's successful, and why. Precisely because of proximity, urban entrepreneurs see more than their rural counterparts. They know what others are making, how they're making it, what they're selling, and at what price.

Cities also foster information exchange, from the metropolitan newspaper's business section to the grain exchange, from specialized business and trade publications to the stock exchange. In cities, a wide range of formal and informal networks form to share data, tips, leads, ideas, names, and plans that direct capital resources to the best endeavors. Rotary clubs, chambers of commerce, trade organizations, banks, pawnshops, government think tanks, university groups, health clubs, golf courses, power lunches all help money find the paths of greatest potential.

George Gilder argues that cities are obsolete in the information age because people can live wherever they want. Futurist John Naisbitt and business guru–*Forbes* columnist Tom Peters counter that cities will thrive in the information age precisely because people can live where they want. They argue that cities attract people because living and socializing in a community is even more important when work is performed on computer screens. Says Peters, "clusters of exuberant variety are at the heart of entrepreneurship and progress. . . . Technology is great, but humans like to schmooze."

The recent real-estate boom in the Chelsea neighborhood of Manhattan has been fueled by the arrival of hundreds of companies designing web sites, stretching the Internet, and then hitting the bars and cafés of Chelsea after work. Creative people need to see each other. The prosperity of the Silicon Valley spread north to San Francisco because young software builders wanted to see something more than a parking lot after work. For such reasons, the Internet won't hurt cities anymore than the telephone did. As Edward L. Glaeser says, "The notion that telecommunication can replace face-to-face meetings defies common sense. Phones have been ubiquitous for decades, but that hasn't stopped businessmen from consummating deals and brainstorming ideas around the conference table."

Cities amass capital, information flow, and business connections. They channel the nation's capital resources toward the most promising economic activities.

Education

Cities also make it easy to educate children, society's future innovators, workers, investors, artists, and citizens.

The student population in a city is both large and concentrated; the number of schools is large as well. Thus cities can provide more opportunities than can other settings to connect students to the schools best for them.

Opportunities are potentially unlimited. A city can sustain dozens of kinds of schools: neighborhood and specialty, language immer-

You Can't Build a City on Pity

sion and arts, Montessori and Waldorf, technical and college bound. Some cities have many of each type of school. Depending on the school system, if parents and students don't like a particular school, teacher, or course, they may be able to choose another.

These options are less likely to be found outside cities. With little competition, rural areas cannot offer as many opportunities. Even suburban school systems hold limited ability to match students with the school, teachers, and courses that will maximize their potential.

The best institutions of education in the world are usually located in cities. The size, diversity, and density of cities create a natural advantage attractive to consumers of education. In the United States, the urban education advantage can clearly be seen in higher education. In kindergarten through twelfth grade, however, the advantage has been smothered by government monopoly of school finance and restrictive and hostile policies toward private and parochial schools. Chapter 5 discusses at length how school choice can allow cities their natural advantage in education.

CITIES MUST REMAIN cities to continue fostering wealth and culture and spreading civilization. If cities unravel, if urban proximity and its efficiencies end because government policy spreads population and markets randomly over the landscape, then the wealth produced in cities dissipates. Crime and poverty fill in where markets have collapsed. As daily life grows more dangerous and degraded, civilization unravels.

This book has two main themes, which I will explore in tandem: (1) the natural advantages of cities and (2) the ways in which the federal government, often in collusion with well-intended experts, has almost systematically worked to undermine those advantages and wreak havoc on our urban areas. It is the greatest American tragedy of the twentieth century that the federal government has been busy destroying its own cities, both by design and by accident, for the last fifty years. This sorry tale involves federal programs for welfare, education, housing, highway construction, and environmental regulations and policies regarding shipping, international commerce, and immigration. In the twentieth century, our cities have not merely been neglected, as many experts suggest; they have experienced an all-out assault.

Corollary to these themes is the proposition that cities have compounded the tragedy imposed on them by Washington. They have allowed themselves to fall into the victim mentality; they have failed to keep their own houses in order; and they have failed to maximize their own advantages even to the limited degree that federal policies will allow.

The good news is that despite misguided experts and counterproductive federal policies, some cities have survived, rebounded, even thrived. They have done so by making themselves as livable and affordable as possible while working to reverse the federal policies that damage them, by creating the conditions in which large numbers of people can conveniently go about their business, by taking the simple but important steps of fighting crime, suppressing fire, protecting public health, creating educational opportunities, inspecting buildings, picking up trash, removing sewage, and delivering clean water. Cities that have done these things well have generated opportunities for market activity and widespread prosperity.

In the balance of this book I hope to point the way toward a new outlook that can help us rediscover the value of cities.

How to Cut Government Spending and Live to Tell about It

TOO OFTEN, elected officials believe that they are involved in a zero-sum game, that every function performed and dollar spent can be cut only at the cost of diminished services. They believe that cutting taxes entails inflicting pain by taking from taxpayers services they need and desire.

This attitude contradicts a concept largely misunderstood by government, but quite familiar to the private sector: productivity. The strategy in the private sector is to produce the quality services and goods that the market wants at lower cost; doing so often results in profit.

The goal of government should not be to accumulate money, but to create conditions under which its people may prosper. It's time for city leaders to embrace this goal. A city that spends itself to high tax levels suffers for it; people with means choose not to live or conduct commerce there. A city with poor services also suffers; people and businesses are repelled by failing schools, rampant crime, and filthy streets pocked with potholes. Attracting customers by increasing quality and reducing prices comes naturally to business. Why can't government do the same?

The surest way to reduce the price of government is to reduce costs. Yet in recent times government has developed the notion that the best way to manage is not to improve efficiency, but to get money from other governments. Officials feel that if they whine and cry and complain, senior levels of government will feel sorry for them and give them money.

Granted, there are legitimate reasons for one government to give money to another. In 1912, for example, Milwaukee and other cities agreed to give up their power to enact scores of fees and tax hundreds of items of property in exchange for sharing a statewide Wisconsin income tax. The change ended a balkanized tax system that interfered with the flow of commerce in Wisconsin.

Still, city dependence on increases in state or federal aid is a poor management strategy. Cities should attract and please customers by cutting costs and improving services, not by shopping for pork. Taxpayers, especially voting taxpayers, support restrained spending and lower taxes. I have found that elected officials who actually practice this restraint—and communicate this practice—can not only please, but delight, their citizens. Other mayors are coming to the same conclusion.

In 1991, broke, busted, and bankrupt, Philadelphia found someone to get the city off its knees. Ed Rendell won the job of mayor. His predecessors Frank Rizzo and Wilson Goode had each in his own way weakened Philadelphia's financial status. Rizzo, a former police chief, had it right on crime—he was against it. But under Rizzo, Philadelphia developed big financial problems, and Rizzo had few answers except to spend money and dig a fiscal hole for his successor. On his last day in office, in a final eruption of spending, Rizzo used the power of executive order to increase city employee pensions by more than 30 percent.

This action set up Wilson Goode to fail. And he did. Goode, a certified public accountant, responded to Philadelphia's fiscal crisis by increasing taxes and spending more than the city took in. Like Boston's Mayor Curley fifty years before, Goode counted on federal and state aid that never materialized. He brought the city to its knees and begged the Commonwealth of Pennsylvania and the federal government for more money. In his book, *In Goode Faith,* he

How to Cut Government Spending and Live to Tell about It

tells of how he finally owned up to the impending bankruptcy of his city: "By the time 1990 rolled around, it was clear that we would not get the additional tax money and I would have to make major cuts in city programs. Much as I hated to, I reduced spending for . . . every single thing I could."

In November 1991, the people of Philadelphia, which was then in state receivership, voted to get their city off its knees and elected Ed Rendell, a candidate who wasn't apologetic about his plans to cut spending. As mayor, Rendell cleaned up the mess in Philadelphia; he cut spending by over $30 million per year, balanced the books, and stood firm during a city-employee strike. At the same time, he was able to improve city services, and it is this improvement in services to which he points most proudly. Ed Rendell rallied his people to express their love and confidence in Philly, and he was overwhelmingly reelected in 1995.

Six hundred miles due west, Indianapolis had never been on its knees, and its populace voted to remain standing. After twelve years of award-winning government led by Bill Hudnut, Indianapolis voters elected another Republican, Steve Goldsmith. Hudnut had focused on public works, the Hoosier Dome, the Pan-American Games, and metropolitan government as ways to keep his city healthy. He was widely considered a tough act to follow. But Goldsmith was not about to be left in Hudnut's shadow. He decided to make Indianapolis even better and took an "if it's not broke, fix it anyway" approach to the city. Through cuts, service contracts, and various other reinvention strategies, he reduced spending and shrank the size of the city's government.

IN MILWAUKEE, I brought to the office of mayor considerable expertise in line-item budgeting. I had been on the Wisconsin legislature's Joint Finance Committee—the budget-writing committee—for over ten years. I was identified as a person who voted to cut spending. I was proud of my record of fiscal responsibility. Cochair Gerald Kleczka, now a U.S. congressman, and I had a good working relationship. We enjoyed our roles of protectors of the public purse.

Substantial though my ability may have been in this area, I soon found it was largely irrelevant to my work as mayor, except in understanding how the Common Council might be thinking. As a legislator, I had viewed cutting spending as an exercise in pruning a tree or cutting back weeds. Government spending was destined to grow and grow; our role as legislators was to keep that growth under control. I cut spending because it was the right thing to do; I didn't look at spending in a programmatic way. When I voted to cut a program, I looked at my vote as tough medicine, as if cutting spending was like castor oil, distasteful but somehow ultimately good for the people.

Then I became mayor; I made the transition from legislator to executive and acquired a different mind-set. I learned that cutting spending need not be painful. Of all the myths government perpetuates, this is perhaps the biggest. The truth is, government is rife with entire systems, entire ways of going about the business of governing, that encourage needless spending and bad service. Reforming those systems enables government to help people rather than hurt them. Such reform relieves, rather than instills, pain.

How Heroic Mayors Spend More

The traditional system works like this. Agencies present inflated budgets detailing their needs, wants, and desires; they request increases far larger than what they know they are going to get. Then, enter the heroic chief executive—the governor, county executive, or mayor. The heroic leader hacks away at the inflated agency requests, points a finger at the agency heads, lectures them about their excessive spending, and with maximum bravado, pares back the budget requests. The process is like a morality play, and it works well as a public relations ploy. It builds the image of the executive as the strong parent who looks over the budget process and keeps the

How to Cut Government Spending
and Live to Tell about It

naughty children in line; the naughty children—the bureaucrats—like the process because it is predictable and nonthreatening. It also gives their agencies more than they would otherwise get while persuading taxpayers that someone is minding the store and looking out for their interests. Meanwhile, spending and taxes go up and up and services are maintained at the same level or cut.

Before I became a member of the legislature, the senate cochair of the Joint Finance Committee was a veteran legislator named Walter Hollander, nicknamed "Half a Loaf." At budget time he would grill agency heads, peer through his glasses at their budget requests, mop his brow, encourage debate among fellow committee members, ask for more information from agency staff, consult with legislative fiscal experts. Then he would almost always cut in half whatever budget increase the agencies had requested. They learned pretty quickly to ask for twice as much as they wanted in order to get a little more than they needed.

The logical flaw in the traditional system is that, under cabinet government, the agency heads work directly for the executive who appointed them. If a governor were looking out for the taxpayers' best interests, he wouldn't entertain inflated, padded, trick-riddled budgets. If a mayor were truly sincere about cutting spending, she would tell her appointees to cut the budgets in the first place. That's what I do. I take far more pleasure in receiving honest, trim budgets from agencies than I do in heroically confronting agency overspending that should never have been proposed in the first place.

In Milwaukee, we skip the part of the budget debate that involves the agencies' submitting their fat requests to be cut by the mayor. It saves everyone time and energy. Instead, the agencies' requests meet their predetermined targets, below the rate of inflation, and the budgets align with strategic goals established by the agency and consistent with the city's overall goal of adding value to the lives of its citizens.

The budgets then go to the Common Council. Since the council participates in the planning that goes into creating the budgets, it generally approves what is presented, but it sometimes finds ways to make additional cuts and improve services. The council focuses on the policy goals and strategies associated with city services rather than on trying to micromanage through line-item budgeting. The agencies, taxpayers, and I appreciate this approach.

Of course, budgeting in Milwaukee is not always sugar and spice. Changing government can be difficult. Reducing spending requires managers to work hard, think creatively, and remain focused on goals. Although it is good for taxpayers, reducing spending is not necessarily easy, and it becomes impossible if the top elected leaders aren't sincere about it.

The public suspects that things can get better and expects mayors—and other elected officials, but mayors in particular—to make them better. So the best thing to do, the right thing and the politically astute thing, is to give the public what it wants instead of making excuses.

Mayors *can* cut spending. They can do it in big ways and in small ways. And when they do cut spending, they should insist that their methods be applied on a much larger scale to state and federal budgeting. Here are some examples of how we have managed in Milwaukee.

Measles

Our Health Department was in the habit of spending more money every year than the year before, even adjusted for inflation. The department, we found, was providing redundant services. For example, it devoted substantial time and money to providing immunizations for children, especially for poor children—an important and needed service. But in the mid-1960s, Medicaid was established to provide low-income people, particularly children, access to health insurance. Suddenly, through Medicaid insurance, these children and their parents could go to their own doctor rather than to the city for immunizations.

How to Cut Government Spending and Live to Tell about It

To protect their jobs and maintain a record of public service, Health Department staff wanted to continue to provide immunizations for poor children. The department arranged with the health-insurance companies for Medicaid-eligible children to receive their shots from the Health Department. This arrangement suited both the staff of the Medicaid insurance companies, who wanted to keep costs down, and the staff of the Health Department, who wanted to keep busy. It also meant that Milwaukee taxpayers were paying twice: federal and state taxes, to provide Medicaid coverage for poor children, and property taxes, to provide immunizations to these same children after their Medicaid insurance companies denied them the immunizations.

Children fell through the cracks. Parents would bring their children to the Medicaid-paid clinics for routine care and immunizations only to be told to go to the city Health Department for the immunizations. This extra step often proved to be just too much trouble. Anybody who cares for young children knows the difficulty of cajoling a child to go anywhere for shots once, much less having to go through the whole process a second time.

When I took office in 1988, the immunization rate in Milwaukee was a startlingly low 23 percent. In 1989 a measles epidemic hit; over a thousand children in the city contracted measles, and tragically, two died. Experts observed that the epidemic was "notable for the size of the . . . outbreak, the severity of so many of the cases, and for the large number of children who should have been vaccinated but were not."

Efficiency expert Peter Drucker says that the key to success for an enterprise is to deliver high-quality service fast and at a low cost. The Health Department was doing just the opposite. It delivered low-quality service (a low rate of service) very slowly (people had to go to two different places to receive it) and at double the cost. To change this, we set up an effective incentive for the insurance companies to provide the service they're paid to provide. Under the new arrangement, if somebody covered by Medicaid receives an immunization from the city, the cost plus a penalty is charged to the insurance company. In addition, the Health Department allocates its resources more effectively, toward immunizing children who don't have insurance coverage.

A local antipoverty advocacy group, the Milwaukee Hunger Task Force, at first vigorously opposed this Health Department reorganization. One year later, the task force endorsed it; the group found that needy populations were receiving better, targeted care. According to the Federal Center for Disease Control, the number of Milwaukee County two-year-olds who received full immunizations in 1995 was up from 23 percent to over 80 percent, approaching our 90 percent goal.

Delivering the Mail

The Milwaukee Treasurer's Office is run by Wayne Whittow, one of the most dedicated friends of the taxpayer whom I've met. He helps prove that by reducing cost, you need not reduce service.

Whittow's Treasurer's Office routinely sent a full-time employee—"the mail guy"—to the post office to pick up the mail. The mail guy picked up the mail for a good reason: checks were in it, and prompt deposit of that money allowed it to earn more interest, keeping the tax rate that much lower. The net benefit of extra interest earnings outweighed the cost of the labor needed to pick it up, process it quickly, and run it over to the bank. This routine was established when the post office delivered mail only once a day. The mail guy became a permanent fixture and had a city vehicle at his disposal.

As the years went by, the U.S. Post Office, in response to competition, instituted custom delivery, delivery to the same address more than once a day. Whittow, always dedicated to saving the taxpayer some money, jumped at the chance to order custom delivery and eliminate both the position and the city vehicle associated with collecting the mail.

How to Cut Government Spending and Live to Tell about It

(No, Whittow didn't throw the mail guy out on the street when his faithful days of lugging money ended; he was reassigned to a position that had recently become vacant through retirement.) Wayne Whittow was able to help the taxpayers of Milwaukee by letting the U.S. Postal Service deliver the mail.

Who Needs Title Searches?

When consumers pay the true cost of a product or service, the cost is internalized. Internalized costs encourage consumers to make smarter decisions. Subsidized products, which consumers buy for less than their full cost, encourage inefficient behavior. For government operations as well, internalized costs encourage efficiency. Here's how it can work.

In the Milwaukee Assessor's Office, seven full-time employees performed title searches, but not for the assessor. The assessor's employees were doing title searches for the Treasurer's Office and a few other agencies. City assessor Julie Penman came to the conclusion that doing title searches for other departments did not help her agency meet its core goal of accurate and fair property-tax assessment. Penman wanted to end the practice. She needed help and she got it. Under the new system of internal charges, costs are assigned to the department to which the benefits accrue. The Treasurer's Office found out it would have to begin paying for title searches from the assessor; its budget would go up while the budget of the Assessor's Office would go down. Adding the equivalent of five or six full-time employees would have a significant impact on the Treasurer's Office. The treasurer and assessor talked things over; looking for a way to provide the same service at less cost. Because the treasurer had to begin paying the true cost of the service, he shopped smart, and together they located a private title-search company that could do the job better for one-third less money.

The former title searchers, meanwhile, got better jobs; they were retrained to fill vacant assessor positions. The Assessor's Office no longer wastes time on something that is not a core function. And tax dollars are saved.

Cross-Training on the Boulevard

Cross-training is nothing new to the private sector, but the workforce in the public sector remains full of stratification. Our Forestry Division, for example, was stratified—literally. People who worked above the ground were called arborists; people who worked on the ground were called landscape gardeners; and never the twain should meet.

Milwaukee has an extensive and beautiful system of boulevards, attractively landscaped with trees and flowers, a real source of community pride. Until I took office, the workers who tended the roses on Layton Boulevard were never the same workers who trimmed the maple trees shading them. Because planting and tree trimming are seasonal activities, taking place in spring and autumn, respectively, an appropriately trained employee could easily do both, so this practice was especially inefficient. It made sense to cross-train the staff of the Forestry Division so that just about every employee could do just about any job.

Some long-time employees were fearful and resistant, but they went along with the change eventually and most ended up liking it. Being able to do more than one thing not only made their jobs more interesting, but opened up new promotional opportunities.

The division realized some unexpected benefits from the cross-training also. Seasonal employees, many of whom are women and people of color, are now finding increased opportunities for full-time forestry work, and management personnel are happier knowing they don't have to read a labor contract every time they want to reassign people to meet a service need.

The Smoothest Sidewalks in Wisconsin

In Milwaukee we had somehow developed a lower tolerance for crooked sidewalks than that of any other city in Wisconsin. If our

How to Cut Government Spending and Live to Tell about It

sidewalks deviated in any direction by more than a quarter inch, a new sidewalk slab was put in place. I imagine that years ago some city engineer and assistant city attorney shared lunch and, in a fit of compulsive behavior, drew up the quarter-inch policy and enshrined it in the administrative rule book.

Smooth sidewalks are nice. People are less likely to trip on them. If they don't trip, they don't sue the city. But how smooth does a sidewalk have to be? How close to perfect? Sidewalks near trees can be pushed out of alignment by tree roots. Should the tree be killed to attain a perfectly level sidewalk, or should we sometimes tolerate deviation to save a shade tree?

The worn sidewalks in New Orleans, buckling from the runaway roots of old magnolia trees, are part of the charm and value of the Garden District. The bumpy cobblestone sidewalks on Beacon Hill in Boston enhance a great tourist attraction. It's the deviations that add interest to the sidewalk.

With this in mind, we did some research and found that less than four hundred dollars in claims concerning crooked sidewalks had been awarded during the previous year in a city of over six hundred thousand people. Most other Wisconsin cities were using a half-inch tolerance standard, and they didn't have many claims either.

We saved money by switching to a half-inch sidewalk deviation standard. Some of our engineers needed therapy when we made the switch, but they're okay now. Even more important, our constituents saved money, since property owners pay half the cost of sidewalk repair through special assessments. There has been no noticeable effect on our claims.

Making Insurance Companies Compete

It is important to bear in mind that the cost-saving measures cited so far, although perhaps most evident in their specific and practical applications, have involved *programmatic* changes in Milwaukee's municipal government. One change that is clearly programmatic in nature involves employee health insurance.

Until recently, the city's health insurance basically paid 100 percent of whatever health-insurance plan a city employee wanted. It was costing us a fortune. Now we make insurance companies compete against each other. Every October, in addition to persuading the city to offer their plans, they need to convince individual employees to choose their plans from among the competing plans.

Thanks to competition, our city employees help save taxpayers money. With our unions, the city puts together a uniform health-insurance package that provides excellent coverage with almost no co-payments. Then we tell all the health maintenance organizations (HMOs) in town, "This is what we want for our employees," and we invite them to tell us, in bid form, what they would charge per employee per month to provide such coverage.

The lowest-bid HMO plan is offered to city employees for free, that is, there are no premiums to pay. The other HMO plans are offered for premiums that reflect the difference between their bid and the lowest bid.

Employees get a wide range of health-insurance options, and they generally choose against high cost and for high quality. Not everyone chooses the low-cost bid. Some prefer a higher-cost plan and choose to pay the premiums. The city's health-insurance program forces insurance companies to keep their pencils sharp and offer low cost and high quality. It has saved Milwaukee more than $5 million in the last eight years.

ISIPing the ISAs: The Language of Competition

Private insurance companies aren't the only entities to experience the city's move to efficiency through competition. We have begun to build competition into the operations of city government itself.

In Milwaukee, as in many large units of government, we had a big problem with ISAs. So we ISIPed them. Let me explain.

ISAs are internal service agencies. They are businesses within government that provide other agencies with services—computer

How to Cut Government Spending
and Live to Tell about It

maintenance, printing, vehicle rental and maintenance, building repair, and employee training. Typically, ISAs are monopolies. Ours were no exception. In Milwaukee's budget, they accounted for about $43 million, or just under one-third of the city property-tax levy. The situation cried out for reform.

Before reform, a customer agency needing a service through an ISA didn't control the money it needed to buy that service. The money went directly into the ISA budget. Most governments still budget this way. This situation is analogous to your needing a new computer and finding that someone has already given your money to Computers R Us. You might need a Compaq with various functions and capacities to do your job, but Computers R Us only sells Apples. And chances are, since they already have your money in hand, you're not even going to get the Apple you need when you need it, unless you're a personal friend of the manager.

That's pretty much how our ISAs worked. Customer agencies were complaining all the time. We performed a quick survey to confirm and document the extent of the problem. We found three things wrong with our ISAs: high cost, low quality, and slow service. Which is everything.

We had three options. We could come up with a new set of rules and regulations that would legislate improvement in our ISAs. But we knew that control systems rarely work in achieving sustainable results. If command and control worked, the Soviet Union would now have the world's most dynamic economy. Or at least it might still exist.

Another option was to privatize, farm the stuff out. This works as a tool, but not as a goal in itself. Privatization as a goal destroys morale, dislocates people, and often backfires. As Mayor Ed Rendell of Philadelphia remarked, "People [i.e., private vendors] do treat the government as a cash cow, as a simpleton." For instance, the Pentagon is the biggest cash cow of them all; it contracts with sole-source vendors who invent ultra-high-cost toilet seats.

Eventually, on the advice of budget director Anne Spray Kinney, we went with a third option—competition. We took a market approach in which our ISAs could survive on their ability, in competition with private vendors, to attract customer agencies. Funding for internal services was shifted to the customer agencies. They were given free rein to choose how to spend it. They could continue to use the city's ISAs, or they could buy the needed services on the open market. We made the changeover gradually and trained ISA employees in basic marketplace survival skills. We called this process the Internal Services Improvement Project (ISIP).

For the first time ISAs, former government monopolies, had to compete. For the first time customer agencies had no one to blame if they purchased inferior services. For the first time each organization was held accountable for its actions.

The first few months were hard for the ISAs. When they bid against private vendors, the private bids were lower every time—from 7 to 121 percent lower. The 121 percent differential is a story worth telling.

The Fire Department needed to paint the inside of the fire-station garages. In the past, the city's Buildings and Grounds Bureau automatically got the money and did the work.

The new system put money for painting in the Fire Department budget. The fire chief asked for bids from painting firms. Buildings and Grounds responded. They offered their usual service: institutional green paint applied with rollers and brushes in November at enormous cost. A private bidder suggested rescheduling the painting for summer; then the diesel engines, which have to be inside in cold weather, could be moved outside, and spray paint, a cheaper and faster alternative, could be used to paint the garages. The fire chief chose the private bid, resulting in savings of 121 percent for the taxpayers. Also, as the firefighters could choose the color of the paint, they now look at such hues as Mediterranean blue.

It didn't take long for the ISAs to wake up. They began to schedule better, reduce costs, learn customers' actual needs, and take advantage of their close proximity to their customers.

After just two years, the surviving Milwaukee ISAs compete head-to-head and often beat out private-sector companies. They've won back much of the business they lost. They take pride in this achievement, and their customer agencies are more efficient because they are better served. Further, because their survival depends on it, the ISAs are infecting other areas of city government with increased productivity.

Managing the Managers

A favorite adage of mine is "The strongest tie is a long, loose string." As mayor, I'm familiar with city government and know where I want it to go. But I know less about specific operations within departments. I appoint people to know the details, and while I expect top-notch performance from them, I also give them as much flexibility to perform as possible.

At budget time I set dollar allocations—usually percentage reductions—for every manager. The managers are free to choose any strategy they wish to meet their allocations. In order for this management approach to work, however, the executive's string, loose as it is, must remain tied. It can even turn into a noose at times. Ronald Reagan's managerial string, for example, was certainly broken during his second term, if it was ever in place at all. While his public relations machine trumpeted his hands-off management style, Reagan lost touch with the nuts and bolts of his own administration. In contrast, Jimmy Carter's string was about an inch long. Remember the *Saturday Night Live* sketch in which Dan Aykroyd portrayed Carter phoning instructions for repairing the nuclear fuel cell of a Polaris submarine?

My department heads know that if they try to trick me, I won't particularly appreciate it. That's when my long, loose string gets tight. For agencies under cost-cutting pressure, two of the oldest tricks in the book are (1) simply not to budget for items they think they can receive on an emergency basis throughout the year, and (2) to propose the elimination of popular and essential services, while leaking the proposed cuts in advance to the press, in an effort to generate a "spontaneous" groundswell of public support for the agency.

Things like that don't happen often in Milwaukee these days. We've begun to share a common idea of what it means to run a city. Because good and talented people actually enjoy a challenge, my department heads are sincere and trustworthy about improving productivity. They present budgets that cut costs in a sustainable way, in a way that allows them to accomplish their mission year after year. They don't drain one-time accounts to meet their budget expectations; instead they make real changes and real reductions while focusing on increased quality.

Peter Drucker calls this approach "continuous improvement." He emphasizes that continuous improvement is the only way for a large employer who is under pressure to improve productivity to avoid the meat-ax approach, now euphemistically called downsizing. Downsizing hurts people and seldom improves productivity. "In many if not most cases," according to Drucker, "downsizing has turned out to be something that surgeons for centuries have warned against, amputation before diagnosis. The result is always a casualty."

One thing that makes it possible to set percentage budget-cutting expectations with good accuracy—to pursue continuous improvement—is strategic planning.

"Strategic planning" is a phrase that can lull even the most avid student of municipal government into deep sleep. If my six-year-old son is still wide awake at bedtime, I just whisper "strategic planning" a few times to him, and before I even get to "outcome measures," he'll nod off. But for an executive who wants to improve efficiency, strategic planning is an *exciting* and even joyful experience. Strategic planning helps improve services, reduce costs, and please taxpayers.

Government has traditionally viewed strategic planning as an exercise in opinions. Managers go on a retreat led by a professional retreat facilitator. They brainstorm. Their ideas are scribbled on a flip

How to Cut Government Spending and Live to Tell about It

chart. And everyone heads home afterward feeling good and forgetting fast.

In truth, strategic planning simply requires asking and answering a few direct questions. Why does our organization exist? What is its ultimate purpose? What are the obstacles to our organization's meeting its goals? How do we overcome those obstacles? How do we get from where we are to where we need to be? How do we measure our progress?

When a mayor and council invest their time in strategic planning, they find that many of the duties taken on by the bureaucracy—such as doing title searches for other departments, keeping the sidewalks obsessively smooth, or running to the post office to pick up the mail—don't need to be done at all.

Strategic planning helps managers rid themselves of the bureaucratic tricks that lead to excessive spending. A favorite ploy of old-line bureaucrats is to spend all the money in an account at the end of the year; then it looks as though the money was needed and the base budget is preserved for the next year. In Milwaukee, an agency's base is no longer the prime focus for budgeting purposes. Instead, we constantly look to provide and improve service at lower cost.

In exchange for our department heads' increased focus on strategic planning, we've stopped piling paperwork on their desks. At budget time they used to be buried under mountains of minutiae; they used to have to itemize and describe every piece of equipment, every purchased service, every cost center, and every position in their department as a way of proving some sort of efficiency. Now we tell department heads we won't pay such close attention to inputs as long as they meet the needs of their customers within the agreed-upon budget as determined by our strategic plan. We have shifted the focus from measurement of inputs to measurement of outcomes.

Strategic planning avoids "gotcha government." Gotcha government manages by waiting for people to violate procedures and then jumping down their throats. It's really quite a comfortable system in a sad sort of way. It's based on rules. There are a lot of rules, to be sure, but if you know them and don't break any of them, you're fine. The incentive in gotcha government is for managers to look busy while doing as little as possible. If you don't try to do much, then you won't do much wrong. If you follow the rules, keep your head low, and pad your budget a little every year, you are likely to get most of what you need in order to continue keeping your head low. When you retire you can congratulate yourself on a good, long career. Some nights before drifting off to sleep, you can wonder what you have ever accomplished.

Gotcha government is safe but unproductive. Strategic planning, on the other hand, includes risk. It is challenging. And it can even be fun. Our city budget process, once fearful and contentious, is now a positive experience, reminiscent of the hard work of a barn raising. City managers see the work to be done, understand the common goals, put their shoulders beneath the beams of city government, and heave until the structure groans into place and adds value to the landscape of the city.

Hats Off to Harry Hatry

We measure outcomes, not inputs, in Milwaukee city government. Measurement of outcomes has been a useful tool in business for a long time. It is natural for businesses to measure, for example, return on investment or cost–benefit ratios, because businesses would soon collapse without positive balance sheets. Governments, on the other hand, take a long time to collapse from bad management, in part, because they can tax, borrow, and beg.

Statistical researcher Harry Hatry of the Urban Institute has been advocating statistical measurement of outcomes by governments for decades. He notes that measuring inputs is what comes naturally to government. If a problem develops, governments usually add money and positions to show commitment to solving the problem. So, if education is a problem, they build new schools. If fire is a prob-

How to Cut Government Spending and Live to Tell about It

lem, they add firefighters. If a budget crisis develops, they add budget analysts. If traffic congestion occurs, they add roads.

Although this approach is limited by the willingness of taxpayers to accept higher taxes, it nevertheless remains the natural course of action for government, because the profit motive is missing.

A real danger of management by input is that it can lull bureaucrats into a false sense of security. "If I do A and B," they think, "then Q (quality) will automatically result." The flaw in this thinking was starkly demonstrated in Milwaukee several years ago.

On the evening of Tuesday, April 7, 1993, I was summoned to an emergency meeting at the city's Department of Public Works. For a few days the city had been receiving inquiries, hundreds of them, about an illness. People were suffering from nausea, diarrhea, and vomiting. Many were convinced they did not simply have the flu. The situation was fast becoming very serious.

As the number of phone calls increased, Health Department officials speculated that something might be wrong with the water supply. Water Works personnel, offended by the suggestion, attested to the quality and safety of Milwaukee's drinking water. After all, it met all federal and state standards, the plant's processes were correct, and the water must therefore be clean.

At the city's request, the State of Wisconsin sent its chief epidemiologist, Dr. Jeff Davis, to help get to the bottom of things. At the emergency meeting with Dr. Davis that evening, Milwaukee Health Department epidemiologist Kathy Fessler argued that the illness was linked to Milwaukee's water. Water Works staff were adamant that the problem must lie elsewhere.

"Who's right?" I asked Davis.

"I'm not sure," he said. "We only have three samples so far. We do have some indication there might be a problem with the water. But we won't know for sure until some time tomorrow."

"Dr. Davis, I notice you're drinking a Diet Coke," I observed. "If I put a glass of our tap water (the ultimate outcome) in front of you, will you drink it?"

THE WEALTH OF CITIES

He hesitated. "No," he finally said.

At that moment I decided to issue a "boil" advisory and warn the people of Milwaukee not to drink water straight from the tap until we could make sure it was safe.

It turned out to be the right thing to do. Later the next day came the proof from the epidemiology lab: cryptosporidium, a protozoa that causes intestinal disease, had infected Milwaukee's water supply. A million people had been spared many hours of drinking infected water. As it was, an estimated four hundred thousand people were struck by the crypto bug, and many became dehydrated and seriously ill.

Cryptosporidium comes from mammal spores, either from wild animals, such as deer, or from domestic animals, including livestock, as well as pets or humans. The spores are carried by runoff into streams and, in this case, eventually into the three rivers that empty into Lake Michigan at Milwaukee's harbor. Until recently, even the Environmental Protection Agency did not believe cryptosporidium was a threat to filtered and chlorinated water.

Milwaukee had also experienced mass outbreaks of intestinal disease in 1918 and 1938. These outbreaks, we now believe, were likely due to crypto as well. To prevent future crypto incidents, a water-intake pipe was extended further into Lake Michigan to avoid the runoff carried by the rivers, a new filtering system has been installed at the water plant, and we are building a water-purification system known as ozonization, widely used in Europe since the turn of the century but largely unknown in big U.S. cities. With these measures in place, our water-purification processes will easily meet federal and state standards, but even more important, we will have gained a good outcome: clean, healthy water.

Harry Hatry believes governments can learn to measure outcomes. A city fire department, for example, could focus on reducing fire-related deaths instead of on how many firefighters, engines, and ladders it has.

In 1987 the Milwaukee Fire Department and the community were struggling with thirty-one fire-related deaths. A committee was

How to Cut Government Spending and Live to Tell about It

formed, fingers were pointed, blame exchanged, and the underlying causes of the deaths, such as poverty, were decried.

In this climate I visited a charred house at North Fifth and Wright Streets. The fire had just been doused. I walked into what had been the kitchen. An eleven-month-old boy lay dead on the floor. Sickened and saddened by the tragedy, I vowed we would do better. And we have.

In 1989 August Erdmann became fire chief of Milwaukee. He had a mission; it wasn't to add more trucks or firefighters, but to reduce deaths due to fire, particularly deaths of children. He set this goal, not only for the children themselves, but also for the firefighters. Nothing cuts through the tough exterior of a firefighter faster than carrying a dead child out of a burning house; it is a very personal defeat.

To accomplish his mission, Erdmann set a goal of less than ten fire-related deaths per year with a simple, but effective, two-step strategy: first, build and staff a Survive Alive house to train children how to prevent and escape fire; second, focus firefighters' attention and fire-prevention efforts on areas of the city in which fire-related deaths were concentrated. In those areas, firefighters visited homes looking for defective smoke detectors and replacing them, talking with children and parents about hazardous behaviors, and working with landlords to make their buildings as fire-safe as possible.

The result has been remarkable. By the end of 1995, just over four years into the program, firefighters had visited over twenty-two thousand homes and installed nearly nine thousand smoke detectors. In 1995 only five people died in Milwaukee fires, the lowest number recorded this century. No children in the focus area died in fires. In 1996 there were nine deaths, and in 1997 there were twelve, still low by historic standards.

Norquist's Law

In a 1994 column Michael Barone, an editor for *U.S. News and World Report,* maintained that President Clinton's 1994 budget in one respect followed "Norquist's law."

"Norquist's law," he wrote, "is named after Milwaukee Mayor John Norquist, a 'new Democrat' who says his first goal is to hold increases in city spending below the rate of inflation."

There are various ways to measure government's performance. My proposition is that, short of war or catastrophe, any government's operating budget should rise less than the rate of inflation. If it accomplishes this goal on a consistent basis, that government is meeting the first basic test of efficiency.

Norquist's law is, admittedly, a crude measurement tool. But what it lacks in sophistication it makes up for in accessibility and reliability. Taxpayers aren't interested in performing regression analysis and accounting gymnastics to figure out if government is doing a good job. They want a simple measure they can apply consistently over time. Norquist's law is that measure.

Over the last eight years, compared with the rate of inflation, Milwaukee's tax levy has shrunk by 21.4 percent, or $31 million. Because these savings were made in the operating budget, the savings recur each year.

To meet Norquist's law consistently, a government must avoid budgeting by crisis. A big temptation—and a big mistake—for governments is to use one-time revenue, such as nonrecurring grants or occasional savings on seasonal items, such as road salt, to fund permanent operations. Since the permanent operation continues into the next budget and the one-time revenue does not, a budget gap develops and then a crisis occurs. To meet that crisis, other one-time revenues are "discovered" and applied; then the next budget gap grows even wider.

My no-crisis corollary proposes that permanent programs be funded with stable revenues and that one-time revenues be applied only to one-time projects.

Not long ago our Police Department needed new pistols. One-time, nonrecurring revenue was available in the form of a federal grant, which we used to purchase the guns. As the guns will last ten years or so, not only did we avoid applying one-time revenue to on-

How to Cut Government Spending
and Live to Tell about It

going operational expenditures, but we used it to make a ten-year capital investment.

A good target for one-time revenue is debt reduction. With the help of city comptroller Wally Morics, we have begun a program to use more cash to replace infrastructure. As one-time revenue becomes available, we can use it to replace sewers or repair streets, reducing our need to borrow and saving taxpayers money in a consistent, long-term way.

Bond-rating agencies like this approach. Milwaukee has managed to improve its bond rating to AA+ or the equivalent with the three major rating agencies. Thus the city is able to borrow what money it does need at a lower rate, which helps to keep taxes down.

I BEGAN THIS CHAPTER by pointing out that a mayor—or a governor or president—can cut costs *and* be reelected. I've done it. But getting reelected is not the main reason to cut the cost of government. We should shrink government to help our cities, our states, our nation become better places to live. There are few surer ways to help people than to leave money in their hands. They can use it. Most Americans work hard for their money. Every dollar we cut from their taxes is a dollar they will likely use for something important to them, such as putting food on the dinner table, buying clothes for the children, paying the phone bill, or purchasing school supplies. To those who, like Oliver Wendell Holmes, say that taxes are the price we pay for civilization, I reply, yes, but for working people, cutting unnecessary taxes can be a form of social justice.

And if a government—and a city government in particular—does things well as measured by reduced costs, lower taxes, and better services, it will attract and concentrate more people and businesses. Such concentration will add wealth to cities, to their citizens, and to the nation.

C H A P T E R   T H R E E

Safe Haven

Cleaning House

CITIES WERE ORIGINALLY FORMED for purposes of commerce, human interaction, and *safety*. Cities protected people from invading armies, outlaws, and wild animals. When frightened, people entered cities for safe haven. Criminals and other undesirables were often banished from cities. Today this scenario has been turned on its head. People leave cities to be safe in the countryside. Now state corrections departments parole dangerous felons into cities, using them as low-cost prison storage.

For too long mayors have reacted to crime in their cities in two ways, both of them inappropriate. Some mayors are blind to crime. They make up excuses about it or tolerate it as an inevitable consequence of urban life. They claim that it isn't as bad as it is in some other places. In this environment, crime can grow so bad that it disrupts people's daily lives; eventually they get fed up and move to the suburbs.

Other mayors, rather than ignoring or minimizing crime, use fear to try to market their problem to the federal government. Their intent is to convince Congress that their cities are overwhelmed with crime and should be given more money because of it. Naturally, they fail. They don't always fail to get more money, but they fail to build confidence in their cities. You can't build a city on fear.

THE WEALTH OF CITIES

Let's take a look at the 1995 Crime Bill, supported by the United States Conference of Mayors and signed by President Clinton. Clinton had already ended the hiring freeze at the Federal Bureau of Investigation; now, after years of deteriorating service, police in Milwaukee are getting good support from the FBI. However, motivated in part by a desire to help cities reduce crime and pushed by the USCM, Clinton decided to do more.

Thanks to the crime bill, a federal government burdened in trillions of dollars of debt borrows more money and sends it to cities to hire more police officers. Like so many other federal gifts, however, this one stops giving. The bill helps pay for the salaries and benefits of new local police hires in diminishing increments over a three-year period. In Milwaukee, it covers 75 percent of salaries and benefits the first year, 50 percent the second year, and 25 percent the third year. The federal money then disappears. And no federal funds are allocated for the substantial overhead necessary to support police officers—guns, cars, training, equipment. A fiscal study of the crime bill conducted by the city of Sunnyvale, California, found that the federal government essentially pays 5 percent of the cost of maintaining each new police officer on the street over a ten-year period. Milwaukee's own figures show a federal contribution closer to 10 percent. Either way, it's not much.

Because in Milwaukee we have managed to generate some level of prosperity and we had previously hired more than two hundred police officers with the city's money, we can probably handle the side effects of this gift that stops giving. In a recent memo our police chief advised that state or federal funding is expiring for fourteen department positions. We'll fund them with local revenue. But I'm concerned about places such as East St. Louis, Illinois, one of the poorest cities in the United States. East St. Louis is thirsty for police. Under the crime bill, the city has hired eighteen new officers and plans to hire five more, a 24 percent increase in the number of police. East St. Louis officials must wonder how they're going to pay for these officers when the federal money goes away. The net effect

Safe Haven

of the well-intended crime bill may be to destabilize the fiscal situations of those city governments least equipped to handle additional costs. A federal government awash in debt shouldn't try to meet someone else's payroll.

Although mayors have typically taken an inappropriate approach to address crime, there is an approach that works. Instead of ignoring crime or trying to attract federal charity, mayors would do well simply to clean house. Some are doing just that, with extraordinary outcomes. Local anticrime initiatives, springing from a populace fed up with criminals, have resulted in nationwide crime reduction.

We haven't abolished crime in Milwaukee, but it is on the decline. Milwaukee, historically one of the safest large cities in the United States, is becoming even safer. *Fortune* recently noted that Milwaukee's violent crime rate is one-fifth that of Chicago. In Milwaukee over the last five years robberies have decreased by 17 percent, sexual assaults by 26 percent, burglaries by 6 percent, thefts of automobiles by 11 percent; and homicides by 25 percent. Many other large cities have experienced similar declines in crime rates owing to their own strategies, but not all urban centers have turned the corner. Perhaps what we've done in Milwaukee can be instructive to others, just as we have found the anticrime efforts of other cities instructive to us.

Crime? We're against It!

In Milwaukee, we've declared our opposition to crime. This might sound unnecessary. Unfortunately, however, many well-intentioned people have trouble coming out absolutely and unequivocally against crime, yet an anticrime citizenry helps other anticrime tools work better.

In 1994 I met with the Drugs/Crime Task Force of Milwaukee Innercity Congregations Allied for Hope (MICAH). MICAH is an organization that works for social justice. Based on the model of Brooklyn Congregations, an advocacy coalition of churches in a low-income section of Brooklyn, New York, MICAH pressures businesses and governments to act. When MICAH's Drugs/Crime Task Force asks to meet with me, I usually accept the opportunity. During this meeting we covered MICAH's four agenda items.

When the meeting ended it occurred to me that we had spent an hour talking about items that had little to do with reducing crime; rather, we had discussed ways to make it easier to protest police misconduct. Police misconduct is certainly a legitimate issue. One excellent MICAH idea was to move the Fire and Police Commission—the citizen board overseeing the Police Department—to a neutral location, away from police headquarters. I agreed to implement that item immediately, while taking the other three under consideration. But, I pointed out, it was also important for MICAH's Drugs/Crime Task Force to come out against crime.

A few months later MICAH responded by putting a new item on its anticrime agenda: opposition to drug houses. But the organization's rhetoric made it sound as though drug houses are some kind of phenomenon that lands from Mars rather than the creation of real people who decide to engage in criminal drug activity.

If MICAH, an active, able organization that operates in a high-crime area of the city, has trouble articulating a strong anticrime position, it may be even more difficult for isolated and sometimes fearful individuals to do so. In Milwaukee, we're trying to help people find the words, and we're starting by leading, by saying it for them.

William M. Bulger, who became nationally known while serving seventeen years as president of the Massachusetts Senate, wrote about crime in his autobiography *While the Music Lasts*. In South Boston, explains Bulger, "on the rare occasions when someone crossed the line into heavy felony, he alone was condemned." "Alone" is the important word here. The felon's behavior was blamed not on family or neighborhood or ethnicity, but on the felon. That individual was made to feel alone. We should take a lesson from Bulger and isolate criminals from the community life they

Safe Haven

disrupt. Criminals are enemies of the community. We need to speak that message loud and clear. Too often crime is romanticized, by criminals and their associates, by the media, even by government.

In the spring of 1993, Kansas City, Missouri, played a major role in the romanticization of gangs. The city hosted a national gang convention. Mayor Emanuel Cleaver, an otherwise sensible fellow, invited criminal gang leaders from around the country to Kansas City. Crips, Bloods, Gangster Disciples, Latin Kings were all invited to talk about how to improve neighborhoods and reduce crime. That same weekend Los Angeles officials wined and dined gang leaders at the Westin Hotel, treating gang members like celebrities. They thought, through some perverse social calculus, that it was the right thing to do. These same gang apologists would likely have been angered had Kansas City or Los Angeles invited the twenty most powerful leaders of organized crime to town to talk about ways to solve crime. Yet the gangs, not surprisingly, brought a decidedly mafia-style agenda to the table.

According to the *New York Times,* the gang message was "Jobs or violence." "The agenda of jobs and inner-city renewal that they put forward is backed by a veiled threat of violence. If you want peace in the cities, they warn, you must pay for it." Los Angeles county supervisor Yvonne Braithwaite Burke was quoted as saying to the gangs, "Keep up the good work. We are so proud of you. We are going to do everything we can."

Many Milwaukeeans, too, fell prey to the romanticization of crime, author John M. Hagedorn among them. Hagedorn wrote the 1988 book *People and Folks,* an apology for gangs based on paid interviews with gang members. Gang members received fifty dollars each to sit down and rap with Hagedorn. He continues to attract foundation grant dollars for his gang research.

Hagedorn's thesis is that gangs are not criminal organizations because only a small percentage of their time is devoted to the actual act of committing crimes. This argument is analogous to saying that

THE WEALTH OF CITIES

Neil Armstrong was not an astronaut because only a small portion of his adult life was spent walking on the moon.

Hagedorn's book grew out of his work as director of Milwaukee's Youth Diversion Project, which was funded by federal block-grant dollars. Like so many federally funded programs, the Youth Diversion Project was well-intentioned; it proposed to lure gang members from criminal behavior, but it ended up elevating their status as criminals.

The Youth Diversion Project held public meetings, often at schools, to inform schoolchildren and the public about gangs, including an explanation of gang signs and graffiti. Some parents who attended these meetings felt that the presentation romanticized the gang lifestyle. Some, such as Marilyn Figueroa of my staff, felt that teaching children gang language was a waste of tax dollars. Figueroa said, "My kids need to learn to read English, not Gang." The Youth Diversion Project presentations reinforced the notion that gangs are powerful and widespread, which is exactly what gangs want everyone to believe.

By the late 1990s, there could be no doubt that the gangs that Hagedorn defended in the mid-1980s as little more than social clubs were always criminal organizations.

It terrifies law-abiding citizens to see their government entertain vicious criminals and ask them how to improve the community. It frightens residents of low-income neighborhoods when their government officials reward criminal gangs with respect. These gangs rob, rape, and kill the very taxpayers the government is supposed to protect. Government tolerance, even indulgence, of gangs also frightens employers of city residents. Harvard business researcher Michael Porter found that "crime ranks among the most important reasons why companies opening new facilities failed to consider inner city locations and why companies already located in the inner city left."

Violent crime should be treated as deviant and contagious, not to be explained or excused, but to be condemned, confronted, and

Safe Haven

eradicated by the government of people who are exhausted from assaults on their lives, jobs, and culture.

IN MILWAUKEE we've added 272 police officers over the last seven years, and we've done it without raising taxes. Although federal assistance made available through the crime bill is attractive, we've hired almost all these officers with the city's money, and we can afford them. We've improved efficiency elsewhere in the municipal budget to allow for this valuable and value-adding service. The people of Milwaukee appreciate their police. We know that more police officers and detectives properly deployed in our neighborhoods reduces crime. That's why, in addition to hiring more police officers, we've also put more of them on the streets. Since not much crime happens behind the desks at the precinct, we keep desk jobs to a minimum. One way we've managed to put more officers on the street is to have them direct traffic.

Like many cities, Milwaukee recently had a problem with teenagers' congregating on downtown streets after school. The merchants didn't like kids hanging out downtown; they thought the teenagers would intimidate shoppers and drive away potential customers. Although most of these kids behaved themselves, the merchants had a hard time convincing shoppers that dozens of loud and very visible teenagers were nothing to be concerned about.

Captain Jeff Bialk of the Milwaukee Police Department found an answer. He reinstated the post officers—the traffic officers—who were made obsolete years ago by sophisticated signals at busy intersections. Captain Bialk figured out that safety is never obsolete. These traffic officers make downtown shoppers, commuters, and office workers feel secure, even though their ostensible duty is to direct traffic.

Today's traffic officers on downtown corners keep an eye on the teenagers more than on the traffic, but the teens don't know this. If they thought the police were there to watch them, the rowdiest ones would feel important and powerful. For all the youngsters know, the police are simply directing traffic, but they have a very calming effect on both traffic and teenagers.

Reuben Greenberg's Advice

One city we've looked to for crime-fighting advice is Charleston, South Carolina. Charleston has become so safe that the residents of over seventy square miles of suburban territory asked for annexation to the city. So far, Charleston has accepted, on suburban request, forty square miles. Charleston is getting so peaceful it has been nicknamed "Saintsville."

Charleston's police chief is Reuben Greenberg. Instead of waiting around for someone to address the underlying causes of crime, Greenberg and his police force attack crime. When guns started proliferating in Charleston schools, for example, Greenberg didn't merely complain about the lack of national gun-control legislation; he bought snitches.

In many urban high schools, one way to gain status is to carry a gun, and to tell everyone that you have it. The more kids who know about your gun, the more kids who will be impressed with your status as a teenage gun owner.

The Charleston Police Department decided to turn this equation around. It publicized the fact that any student who turned in a student who had a gun would get one hundred dollars, no questions asked. As Greenberg points out, there are no better snitches than high school students. Overnight, it became better *not* to carry a gun in Charleston high schools, or at least not to let anyone know you had it. Bragging about having a gun meant losing the gun and getting in big trouble.

Greenberg and Charleston mayor Joe Riley noticed two things about criminals: first, that they're less likely to commit crimes when locked behind bars; and second, that the longer they're behind bars, the older they get, and the older they get, the less likely they are to commit crimes when they finally get out.

Safe Haven

So Greenberg and Riley decided to request that criminals arrested in Charleston be kept in prison longer, the longer the better, preferably for the full term of their sentences. Instead of merely complaining to the State of South Carolina that criminals should be locked up longer, Greenberg and Riley assigned a full-time sergeant the task of lobbying to keep criminals locked up.

Every Wednesday, when the state parole board met, the sergeant was ready and waiting to oppose the parole of any felon arrested in Charleston. The parole board was accustomed to hearing the sob stories of the felons who were trying to get out of prison early—how they had never been bad people in the first place, or had reformed, or had gotten their graduation equivalency degrees, or had found God.

Now, Sergeant Wednesday, like radio announcer Paul Harvey, was there with the rest of the story. He reminded the parole board of the vicious acts committed by the criminals. Sometimes he brought their victims to speak as well. In some cases, particularly those involving children, he brought videotaped testimony from victims.

It worked. In 93 percent of cases in which Sergeant Wednesday intervened and opposed early release of felons convicted of rape, armed robbery, or burglary, the convicts remained incarcerated. Previously, 75 percent of discretionary releases in these categories were granted. Greenberg notes that the longer sentences not only help keep criminals off Charleston streets, but also make them less likely to repeat their crimes for the simple reason that they are older when they get out. For every occupational category except one, men who are over the age of thirty-five are less likely to commit crimes than are those under the age of thirty-five. The exception: lawyers.

In Milwaukee, we've concentrated on the parole system too. The Wisconsin Department of Corrections is conducting some mad experiment with the lives of innocent people. The department keeps gathering data on the question: if an innocent population is injected with dangerous criminals, will people get hurt? The data they gather indicate that the answer is yes.

To battle revolving-door justice, we took the Charleston parole strategy and tailored it to meet local conditions. Our Parole Stop is an initiative aimed at keeping dangerous felons in prisons to serve the full length of their sentences.

A local champion of Parole Stop, Alderman Fred Gordon represents a largely African American neighborhood into which two dangerous sex offenders were released from prison early, one without notice to local residents. Gordon says, "If Parole Stop is not implemented, hardened criminals will continue waltzing in and out of jails with reduced sentences, neighborhoods will deteriorate and flight from our city will occur."

State corrections bureaucrats oppose Parole Stop. It is easier to keep the revolving door going; after all, it has momentum. They argue that keeping prisoners locked up is just too expensive—about twenty-five thousand dollars per year on average.

What does society get for that money? Professor John Dilulio Jr. of Princeton University points to four benefits. Keeping criminals behind bars expresses society's moral disapproval, teaches criminals and would-be criminals a lesson—do crime, do time—provides prisoners drug treatment and education, and protects your sister from being raped or shot by paroled criminals.

But keeping criminals in prison is just one part of the process. We also want to get them into prison quickly in the first place. So with the State of Wisconsin and Milwaukee County, we've created speedy trial courts. These courts have cut the time it takes to adjudicate and convict drug dealers, murderers, and rapists. It's important that justice be swift, that it occur while the crime is still firmly in the memory not only of the victims and witnesses, but also of the offenders.

Policing Communities

In New York, city leaders decided to be against criminals. Mayor Rudy Giuliani was elected by promising to oppose crime. It was a bolder move than it sounds. Four years earlier, Mayor Ed Koch, as he faced the fall election against David Dinkins, moved to the right on crime. It was part of the reason Koch's liberal Democratic base left

Safe Haven

him, and he lost the election. But during Mayor Dinkins's four years in office, crime grew as an issue. Dinkins sent mixed signals on some high-profile violent crimes in Manhattan and Brooklyn, stopping short of unqualified condemnation. He also waffled on quality-of-life problems such as aggressive panhandling. Late in his term Dinkins sensed a problem and moved to add three thousand new police officers, but it was too late. His mayoral opponent, Giuliani, had already seized the crime and quality-of-life issues.

Giuliani promised to reduce crime. After winning the election, he kept that promise. He appointed Police Commissioner Bill Bratton, who helped reduce crime 40 percent in New York City by, among other things, changing the attitudes of the Police Department and the entire community toward crime. Giuliani and Bratton were so successful in their anticrime efforts that they ran into the pleasant problem of how to divide the credit. They could not come to an agreement, so Bratton resigned his post.

In his autumn 1995 *City Journal* article "How to Run a Police Department," George Kelling wrote, "Bratton has made sure that everyone understands the business of the NYPD: to reduce crime—not just a little, a lot." Now this sounds suspiciously like a "just say no" approach to crime, until you look at the techniques Bratton used to reinforce his basic message.

First of all, Bratton was careful about applying the community policing technique that is all the rage in law enforcement these days. He thinks the culture of community policing can get away from a department and start to become a goal in itself, obscuring the real goal of police work, to make life better by reducing crime.

Bratton's predecessor, Lee Brown, had crusaded for community policing, but he failed to keep in mind *why* community policing was good. Getting along with the neighborhood groups, making sure the public doesn't look at the police as a hostile, occupying force, making the department more accessible—all are good things to do, but it's important to remember that they need to be done in order to reduce crime. Community policing is a tool, not an end in itself.

THE WEALTH OF CITIES

One of the basic flaws of a bureaucracy is that it is process oriented. When confronted with a problem, the goal of many bureaucrats is to go through motions, to affect the appearance of action, to conduct the processes that have been put in place to solve problems. If they do this, they feel their goals have been achieved and they can go home at five o'clock happy and fulfilled, whether or not the problem is actually solved. Police sometimes behave like bureaucrats, too, measuring inputs such as block clubs created, meetings attended, beat-patrol hours served, or number of squad cars in service. Instead, they should measure crime. Say what you want, but if crime is up, a police department is losing the battle. Community policing is a process that can insidiously work its way into police departments under the guise of a goal. Instead, Bratton kept it a tool.

In Milwaukee, good officers did community policing before it became chic. On the evening of November 22, 1988, I rode on patrol with Officer James Smith. We responded to a shoplifting call at a central-city mall called Capitol Court. The shoplifter was a thirteen-year-old boy. Although the boy had no record, the store wanted to press charges. But because the courts were clogged at that time, the district attorney was not likely to bring a charge against a juvenile for a first offense. Not pursuing a charge of course teaches a horrible lesson, that there are no consequences for crime. Officer Smith did what he thought best; he took the boy home with the intention of lecturing his parents.

The boy's house was on the 2100 block of North Twenty-sixth Street, a low-income neighborhood. No one was at home when we arrived. Many police officers in that situation would simply have let the boy go; he had a key, and letting him go wouldn't have been against protocol. Instead, Officer Smith asked the boy where his mother was.

"I don't know. She's out of town."

"I really can't let you go if your mother isn't home. Is there anyone else we can take you to?"

"Well, my grandmother."

Safe Haven

"Where does she live?"

"She stays here."

"Is she here now?"

"No, she's at church."

"Where's church?"

"Twenty-sixth and North."

So we got back in the car and drove a few blocks to a storefront church. Wednesday night prayer was under way. We walked in and waited in the back of the church until announcements. Then Officer Smith said he had an announcement. He escorted the young man up the aisle.

He turned the boy around to face the congregation. "Is this young man's grandmother here?" he asked.

Head hanging, the boy saw his grandmother and sheepishly pointed her out. Officer Smith went over and said hello, held her hand, and related to her that the young man had gotten into trouble. She came to the front of the church and hugged the boy, scolding him at the same time. Officer Smith turned to the rest of the congregation and said he hoped everyone would pray for the young man. The minister thought it a good idea. Officer Smith and I left as the congregation gathered around the chastened youngster.

The reason for Officer Smith's action was that he cared about that boy and what would happen to the community in which he lived. He wanted to introduce the young man to the community he had violated and make him feel both shame for his actions and the unconditional love of his congregation. He wanted to let the boy know that what he did was wrong and hurt people, not only in their pocketbooks, but in their hearts.

Broken Windows

Bill Bratton's New York City force also vigorously pursued the broken windows philosophy of enforcement. "Broken windows" was coined by George Kelling and James Q. Wilson to describe a law-enforcement style that concentrates on reducing disorder. The theory is that un-tended petty crimes signal that no one cares and lead to fear, more se-rious crimes, and neighborhood decay.

It is hard to convince a police force with limited resources to spend time on petty offenses. The traditional response is, "We don't have enough police. We have time for only the most serious felonies." But Bratton did spend time on the smaller offenses. His department published and distributed its strategy, as if to make a contract with the people of New York.

> *By working systematically and assertively to reduce the level of dis-order in the city, the NYPD will act to undercut the ground on which more serious crimes seem possible and even permissible.*

It used to be that New York subway-system fare beaters were a nui-sance but supposedly not worth the time of law enforcement. A few years ago Bratton's officers started pursuing and arresting fare beat-ers. They found that doing so was anything but a waste of time. Nearly half of those arrested for fare beating either had outstanding warrants for previous crimes or were carrying drugs or weapons.

At the time of this writing, fare beating is down. Windshield squeegee scamming is gone. Public urination is down. So are the bigger crimes. And tourism in New York City is way up. In 1996, for the first time in sixteen years, more jobs were created in the city than in its suburbs.

Gun Control Even the NRA Can't Oppose

Mayors have historically supported reasonable national gun-control laws. The Brady Bill was popular among mayors, and it is now law as part of the crime bill. But mayors can't let their anticrime ac-tivism end there. The formula has been too easy for too long: call for federal action and pose with Jim Brady when he is in town.

I posed with Jim Brady, too. And I deeply appreciate his courage and commitment in pursuing a great cause. But I know mayors also

Safe Haven

need to act locally to make their cities safer from the scourge of crime. In Milwaukee we adopted a waiting period for the purchase of handguns before the Brady Bill was passed. We knew that measure alone wasn't going to solve crime, but it was a step in the right direction. What we liked about it was that it made it harder for felons to buy handguns. It gave our city one more way, small though it was, to increase citizens' confidence in it as a place to live.

We also kicked into high gear a gun-control measure more effective than any waiting period. It's called law enforcement. Law enforcement is gun control that even the National Rifle Association finds difficult to oppose. To reduce the likelihood that criminals or potential criminals will carry guns and endanger the public, we have established a special unit to confront the problem directly. The new unit combines the former Gang Crimes Unit with the former Criminal Intelligence Division.

The Gang Crimes Unit of the Milwaukee Police Department had gone native. Its officers knew a lot about gangs. They knew the gang talk, the gang walk, the graffiti, the turf, who the gang leaders were, and their activities. They just weren't locking them up.

We needed an approach that would eliminate gangs instead of researching and understanding them, so we merged this unit with the Criminal Intelligence Division to form the Gang Crimes/Intelligence Division (GCID). The focus of this new unit is to reduce crime. Captain Don Werra, instrumental in conceiving the merger, describes the mission: "We needed not only to know the enemy. We needed to target the enemy very specifically, and get out ahead of crime. Reacting is not good enough."

One of the techniques the GCID used to reduce homicides was the field interview (FI), an old and proven crime-fighting technique. GCID officers interview potential criminals before crimes occur; they do not simply wait for crimes to be committed and then react.

For example, a person who is walking down the street with one hand in a pocket and the other carrying an open liquor bottle in a paper bag is a candidate for a field interview. As it is against the law to possess an open alcoholic beverage in public, someone doing so gives reasonable suspicion and can be constitutionally stopped and searched by an officer. A person driving a car without a registration plate is also a potential suspect.

GCID officers take advantage of every legal opportunity to interview and search suspicious young men and women. If they find a firearm, they arrest the person for carrying a concealed weapon and ask the district attorney to bring a charge. A charge may not be brought, as the district attorney has a big case load and tends to concentrate on so-called larger matters. Nonetheless, the GCID officers confiscate the weapon and send it to headquarters, where it is inventoried. If the DA subsequently decides not to charge the case, no further action is taken regarding either the suspected criminal or the location of the firearm.

As Milwaukee tax dollars do not pay for free gun delivery, the suspect has to come in to the station and ask for the gun. In some cases, drug-addled suspects forget where their guns are; in other cases, suspects do not want to show up at the police station lest they be arraigned on outstanding warrants. Many of the guns collected during field interviews end up in the property bin and are eventually destroyed.

This is effective gun control. In 1995 alone, almost nine hundred guns were taken off the street by the GCID unit. Homicides are down. I believe part of the reason for the decrease in homicides is that the Milwaukee Police Department takes guns away from criminal suspects.

SAFETY IS KEY to the purpose and future of cities. Mayors must confront accusations that crime-fighting efforts are somehow insensitive, discriminatory, or mean-spirited. Arresting and locking up criminals—separating them from our neighborhoods—is an act of social justice. Law-abiding citizens living in low-income neighbor-

Safe Haven

hoods, often minority neighborhoods, are most likely to be victimized by crime; their neighborhoods suffer and their jobs are chased away. Such people urgently need safe cities. Cities provide the best opportunities for people to move into middle or higher income ranges. Cities allow people with low incomes to participate more fully in community life; cities provide housing options unavailable elsewhere; cities offer public transportation, so people don't have to own a car to get to work; cities are less expensive places in which to live. If we let criminals overrun low-income neighborhoods, we are destroying the best hope of many people who are struggling to get their piece of the American pie.

Cities were originally designed to be safe, and they continue to have natural advantages in terms of safety. Their biggest advantage is the proximity of many people. If a city is organized and built properly, population density makes it more, not less, safe. Within many cities, Detroit and Los Angeles, for instance, the areas with the highest crime rates are the relatively deserted streets of low-density, dilapidated housing.

People have a mistaken perception that their city is safest when everyone is at home at night behind closed shades and locked doors. The opposite is true: there is safety in numbers. Cities are safer when law-abiding citizens sit on their front porches, walk on their sidewalks, and go about the business of their lives.

With vigilant and assertive citizens and a city government committed to fighting crime, we can, over time, make cities much safer. Safer cities will provide an immediate payoff in higher property values, business expansion and job creation, restored cultural and civic life, and a renewed sense of community.

Successful cities in the twenty-first century will control and reduce crime. Unsuccessful cities will try coping with it and making excuses. We must devote our own local energies and initiative to fighting crime and winning that fight. We can't depend on the federal government to do it for us. By restoring our heritage as havens and protectors, we can restore the natural advantage of cities.

C H A P T E R   F O U R

Work and the City

RONALD REAGAN MANAGED to etch the image of the welfare queen deeply into the American psyche. The truth is, there are many more people feeling checkmated by the welfare system than there are welfare queens manipulating the game.

Take the case of J. B., a single mother of four living in a tidy bungalow on Milwaukee's north side. For years she worked hard to get off welfare, taking a series of temporary and dead-end jobs. Between jobs she'd find herself right back on welfare. Two years ago she finally landed a steady, although low paying, job as a nurse's aide. When she took the job, all support vanished.

For a while J. B. worked the first shift, but her ten-year-old daughter began to have trouble at school as she tried to adjust to her role of latchkey child and de facto after-school head of the household. And her daughter called so often that J. B. almost lost the job.

J. B. switched to the night shift so she could be home for her children during the day. She would have to catch a few hours of sleep as time permitted. She couldn't afford to pay a sitter, much less a child-care professional, and struggled to set up an informal child-care network of extended family and friends.

It was difficult for J. B. to manage grocery shopping, cooking, housecleaning, and child rearing on top of a full-time job and the constant worry about child-care arrangements. Her situation was made even more difficult because every evening as she walked to the bus stop her neighbors taunted her for going to work.

One night J. B.'s oldest daughter called her at work. The girl had gotten up in the middle of the night to get a drink of water, only to find the caretaker gone. J. B. had to rush home, and although the children were all right, J. B. decided to quit her job. The welfare system sucked her back in.

By and large, the people of the central city aren't broken. But the central-city labor market is—smashed to pieces by the government's welfare system. Until recent reform, the federal welfare system perversely discouraged people from working even though studies have shown overwhelmingly that America's poor want to work and want to be self-supporting; they don't want to be dependent on other taxpayers. Government should help people achieve these ends.

The welfare system arbitrarily divided able-bodied, low-income Americans into two uneven groups: to one-third of the poor population—mostly women without husbands and without jobs—it provided cash; the rest it ignored. To those it helped, the government provided exactly the kind of help they don't want and taxpayers don't believe in. And the government penalized what welfare recipients say they want and taxpayers say they believe in—work. The government also penalized marriage, saving, and child support.

The welfare system essentially told people who were able-bodied and poor, "On the condition that you don't work and on the condition that you don't marry, we'll give you not enough to live on, but an excellent health-insurance plan. Then we'll badger you to forgo the cash we're giving you and, instead, look for a low-paying job. When you find it, we'll reduce your living standard and yank your health insurance. Then we'll wring our hands as generations of poor people refuse to buck the system and, instead, adopt as the norm the lifestyle into which we have channeled them."

The system was full of perverse incentives. It not only failed to promote the values we say we believe in—work, family, self-sufficiency, ambition—but it was hostile to them. The system was also hostile to cities.

Work and the City

In U.S. cities, discrimination and zoning concentrate poor people in the city centers and exclude them from the suburban periphery. Thus large cities are likely to include entire census tracts in which over half the residents are on welfare. The proximity that helps create wealth in a natural marketplace helps perpetuate poverty in this contrived economic environment. Huge neighborhoods fall into a cycle of self-perpetuating decline. Children who are poor grow up learning there is no relationship between work and money, no relationship between themselves and financially successful people, and that the way to get money is to commit a crime or have a baby and remain unmarried.

Even more tragic than the loss of neighborhoods, welfare has struck at the very heart of why cities came to be.

Cities are labor exchanges, effectively matching individuals' skills, abilities, talents, and interests with an immense array of opportunities. This fluid and dynamic process is one of the engines that drives cities and fosters the creation of wealth. It is precisely because large cities have huge concentrations of workers and opportunities that labor can be matched quickly with needs.

A small-town employer with a specialized need may have to look long and hard—and far—to find someone to fill that niche, or spend money to train someone. But in a city, virtually any job that needs to be filled can be filled by someone already living there, quickly. This phenomenon is, in part, why cities have thrived and will continue to do so.

The ability to fill a job vacancy, quickly and with the right person, is a source of wealth. It is what employee and employer need, and it allows the economy to function seamlessly and productively. People come to cities to exchange things, and the single most common thing they offer is their labor—their brains and muscle, their ability to create value. They come because they know that in cities their skills can be matched most precisely to a means of earning a living.

Welfare disrupted this process by bribing huge numbers of people to withhold their services from the labor exchange. It stopped employees from seeking work, and prevented employers from finding employees. It clogged the gears that grind out a better standard of life for everyone. It diminished urban wealth.

After recent federal reform, the welfare system is no longer as crazy; it is merely half-baked. In spite of all the pro-work rhetoric, it's still not what Franklin Roosevelt intended.

Presidential candidate Bill Clinton injected into his successful 1992 campaign the notion of "ending welfare as we know it." Republicans and so-called Reagan Democrats heard only the first two words, and liberals took some comfort from the qualifier "as we know it." With Clinton's victory came Democratic majorities in both houses of Congress. The stage was set for change, another Clinton theme in 1992.

As governor of Arkansas, Bill Clinton had been a leader among governors experimenting with welfare reform. He dared to imagine a radically different system that encouraged and rewarded work. He and Republican governors Tommy Thompson (Wisconsin), William Weld (Massachusetts), and John Engler (Michigan) not only tapped into middle-class resentment of welfare recipients, but offered thoughtful, if inadequate, modifications to the Aid to Families with Dependent Children (AFDC) program.

During President Clinton's first two years in office, however, he placed welfare change on the back burner, behind his drive for universal health insurance. It was a major mistake.

Clinton understood that ending welfare required universal health insurance. If people were to go to work in low-wage jobs with few benefits, then government would need to make available affordable health insurance. But the public was only lukewarm to health-insurance reform, especially compared to its intense feelings against welfare.

Further, Clinton's health-insurance initiative was unattractive to congressional conservatives because it was not explicitly linked to

Work and the City

the end of welfare. Clinton feared making such a link because ending welfare was opposed by key congressional Democrats, such as Henry Waxman, then House Chairman of the Energy and Commerce Subcommittee on Health. So Clinton tried to pass health-insurance reform on its own. The effort failed. By the time of the 1994 congressional elections, the health-insurance issue had collapsed, while the issue of ending welfare had not even been considered. The president's party suffered a stunning defeat.

The new Republican Congress, elected almost exclusively from more prosperous suburban and rural districts, viewed ending welfare as both a political and a moral obligation. Republican leaders— Congressmen Newt Gingrich and Dick Armey and Senator Phil Gramm—did not use the modifier "as we know it" when discussing the end of welfare. Nor did they consider universal health insurance a prerequisite for welfare reform. They considered health insurance dead.

The House Republicans acted promptly, fulfilling a portion of their "Contract with America" by passing H.R. 4, the Personal Responsibility Act, and repealing Title IV-A of the Social Security Act (AFDC). They replaced AFDC with grants to states, time limits on benefits, and work requirements filled with ambiguity and exceptions.

House liberals who wanted health insurance without ending welfare witnessed the elimination of welfare without health insurance. Senate procedure and a presidential veto over details slowed H.R. 4. But as the 1996 presidential election approached, the Republican Congress and Democratic president discovered a common interest: delivering on the promise to end welfare.

On August 22, 1996, President Clinton signed the bill abolishing welfare. The president and congressional Democrats had, as Michael Wines of the *New York Times* put it, "acceded to what had been unthinkable." The new system, with time limits on assistance and stiff work requirements, is essentially what the House Republicans proposed.

THE WEALTH OF CITIES

What does this mean? Did welfare really end? If it did, will it be replaced by work? Will former AFDC recipients get jobs that move them out of poverty? Although the answer is complicated by not knowing what states will do with their newfound power, one thing is certain: the recent changes in welfare reform will have their most profound effects in cities.

One real concern to big-city mayors is that states will use federal money and flexibility to feed their own bureaucracies rather than move people off the dole into work. A recent *Washington Post* article on Wisconsin's efforts to end welfare declared, "Running such a system efficiently is no simple task, however. It requires a large and sophisticated bureaucracy. . . . Paternalistic reform is popular . . . but it means continued big government, not an escape from it."

But before highlighting the flaws in the recent federal effort to end welfare, let's go back half a century and look at how we got into this mess in the first place. How many people know that Franklin Roosevelt dismantled welfare twice? He did. In its place he instituted a system of work. If he were alive today, he'd likely do it again. Roosevelt's plan for ending welfare is the vision we need today; cities need states to use their new power and flexibility to carry out that vision, as modeled by programs such as Wisconsin's New Hope Project, discussed later.

Herbert Hoover: Father of the Modern Welfare State

Conservatives argue that cities are suffering from the legacy of Franklin Delano Roosevelt. This is not true. They're suffering from the legacy of the president who preceded FDR and whom he defeated, Herbert Hoover. Cities would be in better shape if Roosevelt's legacy had not been eclipsed by a modern relapse into Hooverism.

Herbert Hoover created the modern U.S. welfare system in the early 1930s in response to the massive unemployment of the Great Depression. When he left office in March 1933, the U.S. government was helping about 19 million Americans through federal relief

Work and the City

programs—at a time when the entire U.S. population was less than 130 million. Hoover's programs were called general relief or work relief and consisted primarily of cash grants; that is, the main thrust of his welfare system was simply to give people money. Although some people who received relief under Hoover's system were required to work off their payments, it was not work in the sense of performing a job and then being paid a wage. Hoover was like the parent who pays his child an allowance and then asks the child to mow the lawn, rather than asking for the lawn to be mowed and then paying for a job well done.

When Franklin Roosevelt came to office he dismantled Hoover's allowance system. Faced with the prospect of widespread starvation during the winter of 1933–34, the new president decided to replace most of Hoover's relief program with a work program, thus ending welfare for the first time. He charged a former social worker from Iowa—Harry Hopkins—with the task. Using money that was already in the relief system, Hopkins constructed in only six weeks the single largest community-service jobs program in the United States. Robert Sherwood's *Roosevelt and Hopkins* describes how, in late October 1933, having received Roosevelt's directive, Hopkins summoned aides to Washington's Hotel Powhatan for a Saturday night work session. That night and the next day the work group "drew plans for the Civil Works Administration which put . . . four million people to work in the first thirty days of its existence and, in less than four months, inaugurated 180,000 work projects."

By the end of 1933, the Civil Works Administration (CWA) had benefited fifteen million Americans through six million new jobs; the number of Americans on relief, which had peaked at about twenty-two million, declined to fourteen million during that same period. The next spring Roosevelt phased out the CWA, his goal of preventing a winter of starvation having been accomplished.

After phasing out the CWA, enrollment in Hoover's welfare programs jumped back up to twenty-five million, and Roosevelt agonized over what to do. Finally, he came up with a comprehensive

THE WEALTH OF CITIES

plan that focused on work as a companion to the larger Social Security system. It consisted primarily of the Works Progress Administration (WPA) and the Civilian Conservation Corps (CCC); cash relief again shrank in size, often serving as an earnings-supplement for large families who were not raised out of destitution by full-time community-service work. A much smaller part of the system was Aid to Families with Dependent Children (AFDC), which gave cash to women with children whose husbands had abandoned them or died. Mothers with dependent children constituted just one of several modest relief categories that the Roosevelt administration decided to maintain under the term *unemployables*. Other categories included the people who were elderly or blind.

At its outset AFDC was broadly accepted. In the 1930s 30 percent of the workforce was unemployed and people generally had large families. Not until well after World War II were single women with children to support expected to work outside the home.

Roosevelt's policy of helping most of the poor by creating wage-paying jobs transformed U.S. society. In the spring of 1935, about twenty-four million Americans received assistance from the federal government, about twenty million through general relief and the rest through very small work programs. By that fall Roosevelt had reduced the general-relief population to about seven million unemployables. Harry Hopkins's WPA put about twelve million people to work, and various other work programs, such as Harold Ickes's Public Works Administration (PWA), employed another nine million.

So, for the second time, Franklin Roosevelt ended welfare for all practical purposes by offering able-bodied unemployed adults wage-paying jobs. FDR's 1935 package put in place public work as its main tool for fighting poverty whenever the private sector failed to produce enough jobs to go around.

When the United States entered World War II, federal jobs programs became unnecessary. Suddenly, anybody who could fog a mirror—and wasn't in the armed forces winning the war—could get a private-sector job. The WPA and CCC were phased out, as was the

Work and the City

use of relief as an earnings supplement. The smaller elements of the Roosevelt system, however, persisted, including AFDC.

The United States emerged from the war with a gangbuster economy. In 1950 poverty was a word that simply did not appear in domestic-policy discussions. It wasn't until the mid-1950s that we needed to think once more about creating a large system to help able-bodied low-income adults. Then, the easy solution for public-policy makers was to look around, take stock of what they had inherited from Roosevelt, and make it bigger.

Unfortunately, what was missing were Roosevelt's two center-pieces—community-service jobs and earnings supplements. What remained were some smaller elements and AFDC. This orphaned offspring of a grand vision grew to obese adulthood for a number of reasons. The biggest reason was pure government inertia. The primary impulse of a government program is self-perpetuation. Left alone, it will attempt to grow until it is perceived as indispensable, then it will grow more.

By 1960 it was clear that AFDC had mushroomed into a monster it was never intended to be. No longer were the ever-growing number of AFDC recipients widows or married women whose husbands had abandoned them. Most had never been married. Because many were black and because the program was still relatively inexpensive, opposition to AFDC failed to focus on valid policy matters and instead adopted racial overtones, a strategy that, it turns out, entrenched liberal support and only ensured the program's continuation.

In 1964, Lyndon Johnson unintentionally facilitated the growth of AFDC by declaring his War on Poverty. Johnson's antipoverty initiative was an incredible political accomplishment. His bold rhetoric galvanized public support for antipoverty measures. Johnson made every effort to associate the package with John F. Kennedy's 1962 rhetoric of "a hand up, not a handout." Yet underneath it all, the basic message of federal antipoverty policy was that the government in Washington would help people who were poor with cash and services rather than, as under Roosevelt, with jobs and earnings supplements.

It was the wrong message, not one FDR would have sent, and liberals and the poor have been paying for the mistake ever since.

The Great Society said to people who were poor that free federal government money, rather than wages from work, was the ultimate means to escape poverty. Taking this message to heart, millions of jobless adults stepped confidently into the new and expanded social welfare system and found themselves encased in permanent poverty. The system provided them neither enough money nor enough opportunity to escape poverty.

More than ten thousand days have passed since Johnson declared that "the days of the dole are numbered." Almost $5 trillion has been spent on welfare, among other related programs. Yet thirty million Americans still live in poverty. It's time to help them and to do it right. We should not simply shrink or reform today's welfare system. It must be cut out, root and branch. We must start over with Franklin Roosevelt's original intent in mind: wage-paying jobs for those whom we expect to work and who truly can't find private employment.

The Song Remains the Same

Federal welfare reform has not met the challenge. H.R. 4, which created the Temporary Assistance for Needy Families (TANF) block grant, does not require that wage-paying jobs be offered to able-bodied poor people. Instead, TANF punts back to the states virtually all major decisions about America's poor.

Under the guise of flexibility, Congress and the president have created a TANF program that dodges the three questions that need to be answered about America's poor: Who should be helped? How should they be helped? Who should be held responsible for outcomes? The federal government has given states the vaguest of missions, tacked a few vague reporting requirements on them, added ill-conceived requirements such as arbitrary time limits, and shoveled billions of dollars their way in the hope that the states will succeed.

Work and the City

States are punished with reduced aid if they fail to achieve full participation of clients in work; "full participation" is defined as 25 percent of those entering the system in 1997 and gradually rises to 50 percent by 2002. State jobs programs can thus fail half the eligible clients and still claim full participation.

Under the TANF block grant most states will do exactly what they are doing now, preserving the core of the current AFDC system under a different name. That is, they will give unmarried, unemployed mothers cash grants, insist that some of them eventually work, but then require them to work off their cash grants rather than offer them wage-paying jobs. The only new wrinkle is that after five years, mothers on welfare will get booted out of the system altogether, even if they have done everything the state has asked them to do.

Perhaps the greatest irony is that under TANF states will find it expedient, even necessary, to hire more state-level bureaucrats. Together, the welfare bureaucracies of the states are already far larger than the federal welfare bureaucracy. TANF will require even more state bureaucrats to track mothers on welfare as they travel across state lines, marry, change their names, or in other ways make it difficult for states to impose the arbitrary cutoff Congress thinks they deserve.

Although most states will use TANF to perpetuate the cash-giveaway programs they already run, some will probably implement new work-based initiatives. A few states might follow the direction Wisconsin has taken under its W-2 program, requiring ex-AFDC mothers who receive cash grants to enter workfare immediately. But even states that follow Wisconsin's lead and require cash recipients to work off their grants from the start will be a far cry from Franklin Roosevelt's policy of replacing grants altogether with wage-paying jobs.

W-2: Welfare Reform Lite

Wisconsin recently enacted welfare-reform legislation, endorsed by President Clinton, known as W-2. W-2 is better than the old welfare system, and it is a better response than most states will muster to the new federal law, but W-2 falls far short of what should replace welfare.

As W-2 is the title of the form that wage earners file when paying income taxes, the implication of the name is that families now on AFDC will work, earn wages, and pay taxes. Unfortunately, the program's name promises something that it doesn't deliver: wages.

The good thing about W-2 is that it tries to end welfare and it does link all public assistance to work—immediate work—by requiring cash-grant recipients to work off their grants in what are labeled community-service jobs. W-2 also provides good child-care assistance and health insurance.

But W-2 remains fundamentally flawed. By Wisconsin governor Tommy Thompson's own estimates, three-quarters of the people covered by W-2 will not file W-2 forms. They'll receive monthly cash grants, as with welfare, and they'll supposedly work off those cash grants under the supervision of bureaucrats. They won't be true employees working for actual employers; they will not be paid the minimum wage or any other wage; they will not pay payroll taxes nor be eligible for the earned income tax credit, which makes available to low-income adults otherwise ignored by the current welfare system a supplemental sum of money based on their earnings.

Under W-2, people working off welfare grants work side by side with workers earning real wages. This situation creates additional problems. Second Harvest, a Milwaukee organization that distributes food to the needy, experienced these problems firsthand.

Second Harvest collects superficially damaged canned goods, grocery and restaurant surpluses, and other wholesome food for distribution to food pantries. Workers then sort the food, dispose of unsuitable food, and pack and transport the rest. This is low-skill work. Second Harvest has used two kinds of workers to carry out its mission, workfare recipients and real-wage employees.

The workfare recipients at Second Harvest have little incentive to be productive, since they can't lose their jobs. They resent their wage-earning coworkers, who must work to be paid and who consequently work harder.

Last year the Milwaukee Jobs Connection managed to place some wage-earning workers at Second Harvest. These employees were making the welfare-to-work transition and were trying hard to demonstrate desire and aptitude for the working world. The workfare-grant recipients made life miserable for the Jobs Connection employees, verbally abusing and threatening them. It wasn't long before Jobs Connection officials, fearful for their workers, removed them from Second Harvest and found them wage-paying work elsewhere. Second Harvest is a great organization that lost out on some good workers because of a government system that discourages real work.

W-2, itself a welfare-reform program, needs to be reformed along the lines of FDR's model. Rather than dole out cash grants, it should simply offer able-bodied participants community-service jobs that pay the minimum wage for a limited time period if private-sector jobs truly can't be found. If the W-2 participant works, the participant should be paid a wage, pays taxes, qualifies for the earned income tax credit, and gets out of poverty. If the participant fails to work, no paycheck. That's the only sanction necessary.

New Hope

The New Hope Project is a work-based antipoverty project designed to meet FDR's vision. It exemplifies what President Clinton and Congress should have insisted on and what the states should create with their flexible TANF block grants. It is what W-2 should be. New Hope was not conceived in the halls of state government or the cubicles of the social-services bureaucracy. Rather, it sprang to life in the fertile environment of a city. A coalition of concerned citizens, community groups, business leaders, and welfare recipients started New Hope as a three-year demonstration project. Generous investment by Milwaukee-area businesses, combined with government contributions, has allowed New Hope to go forward.

THE WEALTH OF CITIES

The best thing about New Hope is that it's not a welfare program at all. It's a wage-based antipoverty program. New Hope gets the incentives right. It helps unemployed poor people get work that pays a wage. And it helps the working poor stay employed.

New Hope provides earnings supplements to low-income workers to raise their incomes above the poverty line. It offers access to affordable child care and health insurance on a reasonable co-payment basis. For motivated participants who can't find work after eight weeks of searching, it provides a community-service job that pays a wage while continuing efforts to move that person into the private sector. Incentives are such that it is always in the person's best economic interest to move into private employment and higher paying jobs. Benefits phase out gradually as earnings increase beyond the poverty level.

Nearly seven hundred participants were taking part in New Hope in May 1996. Of the active participants, 77 percent were employed full-time: 66 percent in private-sector jobs and 11 percent in community-service jobs. Another 6 percent were employed part-time. Many of the others were still looking for work.

According to New Hope executive director Sharon Schulz, "New Hope is different because it understands how the labor market works and how people behave in the labor market. Unlike welfare, New Hope is structured so that if you work more hours or you get a better job you are farther ahead than if you just stay put."

New Hope provides a strong framework for rethinking welfare policy. National experts on welfare and poverty have identified New Hope as one of the most creative and promising models for replacing welfare in the country. But the positive opinions of experts are less important to me than what happens to people such as J. B., who would be able to stay in the working world under a system that rewards and encourages their efforts.

The New Hope Project ends both welfare and poverty in a humane way that keeps taxpayers off the hook. Sharon Schulz points

Work and the City

out that the demonstration will soon end, yet it can live on and spread throughout the United States if federal and state officials are really serious about ending welfare and replacing it with wage-paying work. As valuable as it has been for those it has served, Schulz sees New Hope as even more valuable for the effective work-based lessons it can provide to state governments that are willing to go beyond ending welfare to eliminating poverty for anyone willing to work.

I'm convinced that New Hope's lessons can best be applied to the nation's poor through a competitive, outcome-driven model of welfare reform. The best way to connect the unemployed poor to jobs quickly and to help them remain employed is to revamp the job-placement bureaucracy through competition, so that the best results come at the lowest cost.

The current placement system is not doing the job effectively. Like most government bureaucracies, today's system focuses on process rather than on outcome. It holds no one accountable for results and leaves taxpayers to foot the bill when nothing happens.

For Washington or the states to employ tens of thousands of people who try to help low-income adults find living-wage work but who suffer no consequences for failure or reap no reward for success is wasteful and foolish. Government should make vendors compete for the profitable business of placing people in wage-paying jobs and keeping them there. Ineffective vendors, who don't get poor people into jobs, would lose money and soon get out of the business; effective vendors, who do find jobs for the unemployed poor, would make money. And the more successful these vendors are in getting people jobs, and the longer the average duration of employment, and the higher the average wage, the more the vendors should profit.

In Milwaukee, competition has served us well. The city's own internal service agencies have saved taxpayers millions of dollars by becoming competitive in the marketplace. We have fashioned our employee health-care plan in a way that improves quality and lowers cost by requiring HMOs to compete and rewarding the low bidder with more customers. The same principles—competition and economic consequences for both failure and success—should apply to job placement, or earnings maintenance.

Vendors—public or private, not-for-profit or profit making—should bid on the right to provide the unemployed and working poor a minimum standard outcome, say, an income of nine thousand dollars per year for 95 percent of participants (with the earned income tax credit and food stamps, this translates to a minimum income of more than twelve thousand dollars for most families). Probably the best way to structure the bid is to require vendors to propose a monthly capitation fee, a price they would charge per person per month to meet the minimum outcome. The vendors who submit the lowest bids would be assured the most business; more expensive vendors would be allowed fewer participants.

The eligible population should be randomly assigned to vendors, to prevent creaming of the best employment candidates. Vendors could not fail to serve hard-to-employ or recalcitrant individuals until an arbitrator decided that the individual unreasonably refused to work. Until then, the vendors would be responsible for offering those individuals jobs. Vendors would be required to hire and pay the people for community-service jobs if they failed to obtain private-sector jobs for them. Placement firms have a tremendous incentive to succeed because if they do a bad job of moving the unemployed into good, private-sector jobs, they will lose money. Vendors that consistently connect their clients to the private economy, on the other hand, would profit and thrive.

The program should allow vendors maximum flexibility to use a host of employment tools: community-service jobs, sheltered workshops, job training, child-care facilitation, assistance in claiming earned income tax credits, transportation, and other household assistance. These tools would be wielded either by a lean government agency or by a private entity, in either case dependent on its success

Work and the City

for money. The dollars that now support an unaccountable bureaucracy would instead be used efficiently, to pay for results. The major role of government would be to set standards, let contracts, monitor outcomes, and otherwise stay out of the way.

Crucial to the success of the employment-maintenance approach is expanded use of the earned income tax credit (EITC). In Wisconsin, and in Milwaukee in particular, we have aggressively promoted the earned income tax credit to our low-income wage earners. In addition, an extra $70 million a year in state funds flows to Wisconsin's low-income households through a supplemental state credit. But over $50 million in federal EITC dollars will be forfeited from the Wisconsin economy under W-2. Because 75 percent of the W-2 population will receive cash grants that don't qualify for EITC rather than wages that do, Wisconsin, and any other state that pays grants, will lose out on millions of dollars.

Dovetailing wage-based work with the EITC could provide huge economic benefits to big U.S cities. New York City, with more than two hundred thousand families on welfare, could see as much as $400 million if it implemented a system of wage-paying community jobs for its welfare recipients.

IT'S TIME WE REALIZED that the status quo hurts people who are poor. It devalues them. Both the old welfare system and the flexible welfare block grants, as they are most likely to be administered by the states, are sending the message, "We don't care whether or not you participate in the economy. We'll give you some money and keep you in line with rules while we go about our business. As long as you don't cause trouble, you can sit on the sidelines with your cash grants while the market passes you by."

People who are poor need to participate in our economy and add to the wealth of our society. They need to work for their own sake, both to earn money to live on and because the very experience of work connects people to their fellow citizens and integrates them into the larger society.

Recent evidence from Milwaukee's Hillside Terrace public housing project strongly demonstrates that poor people dependent on government can and will respond positively if given the chance. In just two years, from December 1995 to December 1997, the number of Hillside households with at least one working wage earner increased from 17 percent to 55 percent. The removal of perverse disincentives under both welfare and public housing rent policy led to this improvement.

Society needs poor people to improve their lives by working in real jobs, earning wages, and paying taxes. We all benefit when people are able to escape poverty and when they become enriched through work. The benefits to society are particularly noticeable in cities. Cities are the mighty economic engines that provide power for the entire nation. Welfare is throwing sand in those engines. Unlocking the labor market so that citizens who are poor can go to work will help the cities they inhabit grow rich again.

C H A P T E R   F I V E

The Best Schools

"As Suburban Nests Empty, Couples Flocking to the City." The headline in the November 4, 1996, edition of *USA Today* describes a happy trend for cities. Attracted by the convenience, culture, and excitement of cities, middle-aged, middle-class couples are returning to urban living. On reflection, though, an unsettling question attends this headline. Why "couples," that is, why aren't families with schoolchildren returning to cities?

Of all the challenges facing large cities—crime, poverty, schools—it is the challenge of the schools that seems most intractable. Better law enforcement and more efficient courts can reduce crime. Steady economic growth in the 1990s has restored some of the most stressed older cities. But poor-quality elementary and secondary education stands out as an enduring negative element.

Author David Rusk contends that "inner-city neighborhoods can be repeopled with middle class households *without* children if neighborhoods are made safer. Reattracting middle class households *with* children . . . *requires dramatic improvement in schools* [emphasis mine]." Real-estate agents rarely attempt to show city homes to affluent adults who have children. And prospective home buyers don't even bother to ask how the schools are in big cities; they already know the answer.

Presidents, governors, mayors, city councilors, even school-board members know, too, and they've tried to fix the problem. Centralization, decentralization, specialization, mainstreaming, busing, magnet

83

schools, Head Start programs, early education, consolidation, conversion of schools from kindergarten-through-grade-eight facilities to junior high then to middle schools and eventually back again, Goals 2000, multicultural education, bilingual education, and, most recently, School to Work have all been tried. Some reforms have brought minor success, some have had little impact, and some have been harmful. Together, however, all these reforms have not stopped, and may have accelerated, a general decline in educational quality in big cities over the last thirty years. The reforms have disappointed education experts, but more important, they have disappointed parents.

What parents want is the opportunity to select a good school for their children. Choice adds crucial value to our cities. One school that gives parents a choice is the school run by Emmaus Lutheran Church in Milwaukee's central city. At Twenty-eighth and Chambers, Emmaus is in the heart of a low-income African American neighborhood. Almost all its fifty-four students are African American and more than half their families receive public assistance. Although the school provides financial help with tuition, it asks all families to pay something, no matter what their economic circumstances, so that they will be invested in the school's success.

The Emmaus School gives the parents what they want for their children, an education in a peaceful setting near their homes. Children attending Emmaus learn to read, write, do math, and behave themselves. Emmaus also ministers to their spiritual needs. The school requires its students to learn about Lutheranism. It requires them to go to church every Sunday. It also requires the parents to go to church at least once a month. Emmaus is a Missouri Synod Lutheran church. Its doctrine, conservative and fundamentalist, bothers some people, but it does not bother the parents of Emmaus students. These parents know that there are far greater threats to their children than Lutheranism.

"Emmaus has been here since 1890, and we've always been dedicated to serving all of God's people," says Pastor Marvin Ahlborn,

The Best Schools

who runs the school. "We are especially concerned with helping children achieve a richer material and spiritual life."

IF GOVERNMENT DIDN'T HAVE a monopoly on educational financing, more city parents would have the opportunity to choose schools, both public and private, like Emmaus, where children learn well in a safe and wholesome environment.

About nine hundred students and their parents in Milwaukee have been liberated from the publicly financed school monopoly. They can leave the public system at no financial penalty to attend a school of their choice; if still dissatisfied, they can choose yet another school. This system gives parents—who care about their children far more than bureaucrats possibly can—the ability to select for a good school or against a bad school.

On April 27, 1992, in the basement of Holy Spirit Catholic Church on South Thirty-first Street, I met with a hundred worried parents, members of the Near South Side Catholic Schools Association. Near South is a working-class neighborhood whose ethnic mix has changed slowly from Polish and German to Mexican, Hmong, and African American. Schools such as St. Adalbert, St. Josephat, St. Matthew, and St. Vincent were in tough financial shape. Some, such as St. Hyacinth and St. Cyril, were closing; others were on the brink of closing. The parents, few of whom had much money, had scraped together what they could to keep the schools open, but it wasn't going to be enough.

I asked them to keep alive the hope that school choice would soon extend to parochial schools. We had already won the battle for the option of nonsectarian private schools.

"I'm not Catholic, but I know Milwaukee would be a poorer place if not for Catholic schools," I said. "Not only are they good for the Catholic families, they are good for any neighborhood they are in, and they are good for the public schools. Doerfler public elementary school near my house is a good school in large part because three parochial schools are nearby."

That fall I met with Governor Tommy Thompson's budgetary office to encourage support of the expansion of choice to parochial schools. Thompson wasn't ready to move in the 1993 budget, but he was in 1995. His initiative passed. Now the expansion of choice to parochial schools is being challenged in the courts; it was blocked at the circuit court level and is currently being reviewed by the state supreme court. Milwaukeeans can take heart from the fact that school choice extending to parochial schools has already been established in Cleveland, Ohio.

FIFTEEN YEARS AGO I shared the view that vouchers would cripple the public schools and that allowing city students with caring parents to attend the school of their choice would hurt those left behind. But the truth is, under the traditional government monopoly in education, children from affluent families are leaving children from less-affluent families behind. Instead of choosing an alternative school for their children, wealthy parents are choosing an alternative place to live, the suburbs. Vouchers would give all parents a similar power of choice, one that doesn't require moving out of town.

A major factor in the extreme separation of rich and poor in the United States is that people who are rich avoid city schools. Some legislators want to try to remedy this situation through tax-base equalization, in which state governments supplement local tax revenues in poor school districts while withholding aid from wealthy districts.

In *Savage Inequalities,* author and school-choice opponent Jonathan Kozol compares per pupil expenditures in rich and poor school districts—poor Chicago and wealthy New Trier, Illinois; New York City and Great Neck, New York; Camden and Princeton, New

The Best Schools

Jersey. In each case, spending per pupil in the wealthy district substantially exceeds that in the poor district. With greater property values per pupil in the affluent districts, a smaller tax effort (lower tax rate) produces abundant revenue, whereas in the poor districts, higher tax rates yield lower revenues per pupil.

Equalization of property-tax bases is a worthwhile goal. Government should attempt to even out the financial power behind the education of our children. A child should not be denied quality by accident of birth. However, most research shows that spending per pupil is not the determinative factor in pupil performance, or in people's selection of a school. Milwaukee public schools (MPS) spend more than the state average per pupil and more than some suburbs, yet most wealthy and middle-class people with children—including more than half of MPS schoolteachers with school-age children—avoid them.

Kozol's support for equalization doesn't address the fundamental problem of urban public schools: they do not satisfy the needs of parents and children. To Kozol, more money for poor districts is the answer; he doesn't mention better school performance and greater teacher accountability. Perhaps he believes that low-income parents are not inclined or equipped to exercise choice. Yet the popular demand among low-income parents in Milwaukee and Cleveland, the two cities with school choice in place, contradicts that assumption.

Polly Williams, a former welfare mother turned Democratic state legislator, is a champion of school choice in Milwaukee. As a single mother raising four youngsters on and off public assistance, Williams scratched and saved to send her children to private schools through the eighth grade. She couldn't afford private high-school tuition, so her children attended public high school.

When she was informed in 1978 that her daughter would be bused across town, Williams balked. To her, forced busing meant exchanging a bad school nearby for another far away. She requested an exemption. It was rejected. Several nights later, she went to the school board to make an appeal. She lost. Williams strode through the building to the superintendent's office, picked up his pen and notepad, penned a letter, and placed it in the center of his desk.

"My name is Polly Williams, and I live on Burleigh Street," she wrote. "My daughter will stay home before I'll let her be bused. You may send the police to arrest me." Williams was not arrested, and the transfer request was finally approved.

Years later, as a member of the state legislature, Williams heard frequent complaints from parents wrestling with a school system that seemed not to care. "Most parents won't fight," she says. "They don't know how, or they can't. I'm a fighter. I decided I could win the battle for them."

Williams wrote a school-choice bill in October 1989 and spread the word. In less than a year she mustered an unusual coalition of Democrats and Republicans to push her bill through the Wisconsin legislature. Governor Thompson signed it into law, and now one-half the amount of per pupil aid the state gives to schools, about three thousand dollars, is available to nearly a thousand parents to send their children to private schools. Two limitations significantly restrict the program. Parochial schools are not eligible, which means that the approximately five-thousand vacant slots in those schools are not available to parents who rely on the choice program. Also, vouchers are restricted to children of parents whose household income is under twenty-eight thousand dollars. As I mentioned earlier, the exclusion applying to parochial schools was repealed in 1995, but the repeal remains tied up by litigation.

The notion of choice frightens many who make their living in public education. It seems strange that they should so strongly oppose the ability of parents to control where their children go to school.

Because their services would be in greater demand, effective teachers should not fear choice. For bureaucrats, however, the fear is justified. Fewer administrators will be needed at federal, state, and school-district levels. Perhaps this is why so many bureaucrats try to shift the focus of the school-choice debate from parental power to

The Best Schools

the inputs of the public system—money, buildings, staff, special services, anything or everything that avoids direct accountability to parents. These defenders of the status quo focus on the deficiencies of private schools. "Parents might like them, but they don't meet public standards" is a line often heard.

The attempt to refocus away from parental power reaches a fever pitch when the discussion turns to church-affiliated schools. A frequent charge made against school choice is that government funds will be used by some parents to send their children to parochial schools. I have two answers to that charge: (1) Yes. (2) So what?

What's wrong with parents freely choosing to send their children to an accredited religious school if that's what they really want? What's wrong with parents enrolling their children in a Catholic or Protestant or Jewish or Muslim school if they believe it is for the best? Not being able to read at all is a much greater problem for children than is reading from scripture. Some argue that allowing parents to choose religious education constitutes a threat to religious freedom. Yet parents who object to religious education can choose a school that doesn't offer it, and those who want religious instruction would be free to choose a school that does.

In higher education we already have school choice. Pupils can enroll in all sorts of schools at public expense. Using the G.I. Bill, Pell grants, and various other government loans, millions of Americans have been educated at public, private, and religious colleges and universities. A student can use the G.I. Bill or a Pell grant at Georgetown to become a priest or at Yeshiva University to become a rabbi. A student can even use grants at the University of Wisconsin . . . and become an atheist.

The G.I. Bill has been around since World War II and it hasn't hurt public universities one bit. To the contrary, the system of colleges and universities in the United States is recognized as the very best in the world. People come from around the globe to attend the University of Chicago, Northwestern, De Paul, Loyola, the University of Illinois at Chicago, and other institutions of higher learning, but few come to enroll in Chicago's public schools for kindergarten through twelfth grades. Why? Well, for one thing, because they are a monopoly, Chicago public schools have little incentive to make themselves appealing to new students.

Other publicly funded programs in the United States allow choice. Medicaid participants can go to public, private, or religious health-care institutions. People can use food stamps at any grocery store in the United States. These government programs encourage participants to exercise their free choice in the marketplace. The government should do the same with education.

Pretending Choice Away

If the government monopoly of school finances is bad for the United States, it is even worse for our central cities.

Almost every major city in the United States boasts a rich array of universities. Metropolitan Boston includes eleven major universities, Harvard and MIT among them. New York City hosts Columbia, NYU, the City University of New York, Fordham, and dozens more colleges and universities throughout the metro area. Milwaukee has ten colleges and universities, which add enormous value to the culture and economy of the city. How sad that we have taken similar choice and variety, so natural to cities, away from our kindergarten-through-twelfth-grade educational institutions.

This lack of choice particularly hurts students from low-income families. Affluent families can afford to live in any school district or to pay the tuition of a private or parochial school. I do not begrudge them their money or their choice to do with it what is best for their children. Bill and Hillary Clinton, for example, had a choice as parents. When they moved to the White House, they could have chosen to send daughter, Chelsea, to public school. Asked why he sent his daughter instead to Sidwell Friends School, a parochial school, president and parent Bill Clinton replied, "As parents, we believe this decision is best for our daughter at this time in her life

The Best Schools

based on our changing circumstances." Spokesperson George Stephanopoulos elaborated further: "What they did was choose, as a family, Sidwell Friends, and it's a good choice." And it's a good answer. The Clintons were simply doing what was best for their child.

That right ought to belong to all parents. Yet educational opportunity is starkly different for a family with two children and an income of ten thousand dollars. Berkeley professor of law John E. Coons believes that school choice is "an instrument of distributive justice." To ensure that resources are distributed more fairly, we need to put more consumer power into the hands of those who currently lack it. Why school choice succeeds is no mystery. It gives power to the people who have the most at stake: parents.

Low- and middle-income parents struggle hard against a system that denies them choice. Government schools that serve poor communities feel no real pressure to please their captive customers. Instead, they are concerned with self-perpetuation. Their employees are trapped in a situation that they know is wrong but are afraid to change. Taxpayers, meanwhile, respond to the inevitable failure of the monopoly by closing their wallets, which makes school employees even more afraid to take risks.

It doesn't have to be this way. It isn't this way in other parts of the world. Canada and most of western Europe offer a much richer variety of choices to their parents and children. In the Netherlands, Norway, Luxembourg, Belgium, Denmark, France, and Sweden parents can send their children to accredited nongovernment schools without financial penalty. In these countries families in all income groups enjoy an array of educational choices approaching what is available only to the wealthiest families in the United States. Because our system squashes choice, education in kindergarten through grade twelve in the United States is among the worst in the developed world. The lack of competition also hurts private and parochial schools in the United States. By maintaining a level of quality that is merely mediocre compared with that of schools in other advanced nations, private and parochial schools attract refugees from the public schools. If public schools improved, private and parochial schools would have to meet the challenge, as they have in higher education.

Count Day

The exercise of choice in the marketplace is the one thing that gives consumers power. The choiceless low-income children in our central cities are often treated as though they have no value to the school districts in which they live, except for one day a year. On that day, these children are special. Is it the first day of school? The day before midwinter vacation? Some sort of student appreciation day? No. It's Count Day, the third Friday in September. It's the day the state of Wisconsin counts students for purposes of calculating school aid.

On that day, school districts count attendance very carefully. Many go to great lengths to attract more children to school so they can be counted. They offer a fun menu for lunch, or special entertainment activities, or celebrity guests. One Milwaukee high school offers door prizes to randomly selected students. A middle school cancels the final period of classes and hosts a dance "to say thank you" to the kids. According to the Student and Parent Services office of MPS, school personnel go to the homes of children who are habitually truant to persuade them to attend and be counted on that day. On Count Day, children mean money; they literally add value to their central-city schools. On every other day, a central-city child's value to the school is often calculated as a net debit, an incurred cost.

School choice will put vouchers—the power of money—in the hands of the parents of these children who now mean so little. Whether the voucher is $4,200, as in the Milwaukee Choice program, or some other amount, schools wanting that money will have to attract and keep the interest of those children and parents. Schools will have to compete for those children not just on enrollment day, but every day, all year. Parents will know that their decisions matter, that

The Best Schools

the schools want to enroll their children and want them to stay. The schools will attract money only by convincing parents they will teach the children well, and only by delivering on that promise will the schools be able to prosper.

A System of Bureaucrats

I place blame on the educational system, not on the individual people in the system. I oppose bureaucratic rules, not teachers. I feel that teachers, like parents and students, are coerced participants in public education's bureaucratic monopoly. Even the administrators, most of whom are former teachers, have been sucked into activity unsatisfying to parents or themselves. Unfortunately, they feel attacked and end up trying to defend the very system that obstructs their ability to teach to their creative potential. Not having tasted choice, they don't realize how limited they are by monopoly and bureaucracy.

In *Politics, Markets and American Schools,* John E. Chubb and Terry M. Moe argue that education is, above all, political. Bureaucratization, for all its flaws, is not the fault of the bureaucrats themselves. They are pawns in a bigger game being played by politicians, and they are behaving completely naturally within the framework provided.

Bureaucratization is a natural result of efforts by those who wield political power to impose higher-order values on a large social organization. In the United States, these higher-order values are commonly called democratic values. Exactly what constitutes democratic values changes according to who happens to have the most political power at any given time. Goals become confused as schools are asked to provide sex education, psychological counseling, socialization of immigrants, vocational training, desegregation, and bilingual education in addition to "academic excellence."

Under a system of choice, schools can offer what parents—consumers—want. Values are one of a number of factors parents take into account when choosing a school for their child. In big cities, parents could choose ethnocentric education, whole-language programs, or multicultural studies. My guess is that most parents are likely to choose schools in which students strive for academic achievement in math, language, and science. Testifying at a recent public meeting in Milwaukee, Valerie Johnson, an African American and mother of five, stated, "Ideally, what we want for our children is a school environment that is safe, provides challenging academics, and will be an extension of what we teach at home."

Above all, schools should be dedicated to the success of their students. Anything else is secondary.

Liberating Teachers

I'm convinced that empowered parents and students would make good teachers more, rather than less, important and valuable and would make their jobs easier rather than harder. Teachers, more than anyone else except the students, are likely to gain the most from choice. Good and excellent teachers would find themselves in great demand under a choice system.

School choice is rooted in common sense. Most of us see each day how competition spurs achievement—in science, commerce, industry, athletics, even art. Choice challenges the complacency and stagnation of the public-school monopoly.

Protected against competition, the public-school bureaucracy is insulated from accountability. Our children have little prospect for improvement because our schools face no penalty for failure. In fact, the bureaucracy rewards failure. Every sign of declining school performance becomes just one more reason to increase school funding, even though, according to Rochester University professor of economics Eric A. Hanushek, "there is little systematic relationship between school resources and school performance."

Just as the current system imposes no penalty for failure, it offers no reward for success. Within this system incompetent teachers can

The Best Schools

hide, lazy teachers can get by, but the vast majority of teachers—the good teachers—struggle to swim against the tide. Some succeed despite the system, but others become frustrated by a system that rewards failure.

It is fairly common these days for educators to leave the public schools to teach in private or parochial schools. Although they earn significantly less money, they gain freedom and the ability to participate in the miracle of education. The majority of public-school teachers, of course, remain in the system and call for internal changes—higher salaries and smaller class sizes, in particular. More pay and a lighter workload can make teachers happier and, in a small way, improve student performance. Studies have shown that smaller classes have a marginally positive effect on student performance, such a small effect, in fact, that taxpayers can raise valid questions about efforts to reduce class size. Hanushek notes that "econometric and experimental evidence shows that across-the-board reductions in class size are unlikely to yield discernible gains in overall student achievement." Such traditional reforms nibble at the margins, but are far from the answer.

Public-school teachers want more energy and resources focused on the classroom because that's where they and the students are located. It makes good sense, but it isn't happening. Archdiocese figures suggest that there are forty times more bureaucrats per student in the Milwaukee public-school system than in the Milwaukee Catholic schools. Researcher David Harmer found that "in Milwaukee, twenty-six cents of every school dollar goes to teacher salaries, benefits, classroom supplies, textbooks, materials, and furniture. The balance—three-quarters of the entire budget—goes to maintenance, staff, administration, and transportation."

This organization is top-heavy because monopolies, instead of being committed to serving customers through their service representatives (in this case, teachers), tend to define their customers as problems. Before deregulation, for example, phone companies called their customers ratepayers. Under the new competitive system, people have suddenly become customers and are courted enthusiastically. Imagine your child being courted—essentially recruited—by public and private schools much as college students are recruited. Imagine good teachers being recruited by schools managed by principals who recognize that their own well-being depends on satisfying the needs of students and the hopes of parents.

In the government monopoly of public schools, the bureaucracy focuses on finding problems; it perpetuates itself by identifying and spending money on more problems. This process conveniently distracts the bureaucrats from the business of serving customers, which they don't do particularly well. In Wisconsin, the number of children labeled "learning disabled" has more than tripled over the last twenty years. More resources move up the ladder from the classroom as special, bureaucracy-intensive services are created to treat special problems. Granted, some new services are necessary, but all are not.

Today in Wisconsin "learning disabled" includes children who are failing to learn for no clear reason. State statute mandates a specialty-education program for these students, called "gray area" children, who fall somewhere between "gifted and talented" and "learning disabled." At this rate, we will soon have a special "non–learning disabled" program.

As a result of these added programs, even though school spending grows faster than inflation, teachers are losing resources from the classroom. And we know that successful schools keep resources in the classroom. Clarke Street School and Hi-Mount School, successful public elementary schools in the heart of Milwaukee, chose not to have computer centers—a computer instructor and computers banked in a room somewhere. Unlike most public elementary schools, these two schools have a few computers in every room, integrated into the moment-by-moment process of education. The same philosophy should apply to other educational resources; the money and energy should be put as physically near the students as possible, and it should stay put. Most private schools cannot afford

The Best Schools

to do otherwise. The scarce resources they have tend to end up in the classroom by necessity.

Many teachers, through their own abilities and idealism, manage to teach effectively in spite of the constraints of the public-school system. But educating our children is too important to be left to the goodwill of those who teach them. A good education should be built into the very system itself as an inevitable consequence.

And it can be. Moe and Chubb performed a statistical analysis of dozens of educational inputs and found three controlling factors in student achievement. The first two are not surprising: family background and individual capability. Schools cannot directly control these factors. What is the third, the single most important educational input that a school can control? The economic resources of the school? Class size? Teacher salaries? School size? Course work? Time on task? No. The researchers came to the startling conclusion that school organization matters supremely. Far more than any other factor, the structure of the school—who holds power, who makes decisions, and for whom the decisions are made—determines whether a school is effective in helping students succeed. "Choice is a self-contained reform with its own rationale and justification. It has the capacity *all by itself* to bring about the kind of transformation that, for years, reformers have been seeking to engineer in myriad other ways."

THROUGHOUT WORLD HISTORY, for most goods and services markets have worked best in cities. Education should succeed in cities where a rich array of educational choices will do more than improve urban education. School choice will also make big cities places where parents *want* to live. In May 1996, *USA Today* published an article on housing values in the Milwaukee area. It compared a house on Milwaukee's east side with a house less than a half mile away in the suburb of Shorewood. In every way possible, including the relative safety of the neighborhoods, the houses and locations were comparable. Yet the article indicated that the house in Shorewood would sell for twenty thousand dollars more than its twin on Milwaukee's east side. Why? According to *USA Today* the Shorewood house had a higher value because it was not within the boundaries of the Milwaukee public school system.

A choice system would help reverse that equation for Milwaukee and for other big cities. If parents are allowed the power to choose the education that is best for their children, cities, with all their diversity, will hold advantages over suburbs as desirable living places for people with school-age children. Because Milwaukee is the biggest and most diverse marketplace in Wisconsin, it could offer the broadest array of options.

Only in the center of a metropolitan area can we offer people a full range of educational choices. Just as cities are centers of finance, industry, art, and culture, and just as cities are centers of higher education, so could cities be centers for quality education in grades kindergarten through twelve. School choice would eliminate artificial constraints and unlock the value of cities.

CHAPTER SIX

How the Government Killed
Affordable Housing

WHEN I CONSIDER what has happened to U.S. cities over the last
fifty years, when I consider the destructive impact of federal programs—grossly excessive road building, the elimination of most
trains and transit, FHA-subsidized suburbanization, and other in-
ducements to sprawl, when I consider the resulting social chaos and
confusion, as the son of a Presbyterian minister I turn to the first
chapter of the Lamentations of the prophet Jeremiah:

> *How lonely sits the City that was full of people.*
> *How like a widow she has become.*
> *She that was great among nations.*
> *Princess among provinces has become tributary.*
> *She weeps bitterly in the night.*
> *Tears on her cheeks.*
> *Among all her lovers she has none to comfort her.*
> *All her friends have betrayed her.*

In 1965 the federal government did what it often does when it
creates suffering. It grew a new bureaucracy named after the problem it created. In this case it created the Department of Urban
Development—*urban* as in urban problem, urban dilemma, urban
distress, urban decline, urban decay, and, ultimately, urban death.

President Johnson was set to announce the creation of the Department of Urban Development when someone in public relations tried out the acronym, DUD. The name was changed to the Department of Housing and Urban Development, or DHUD. Simplified to HUD, it shared the name of a popular 1963 movie starring Paul Newman and Melvyn Douglas.

HUD got off to a fast start. What it lacked in focus it made up for in size. It grew and grew, and when Ronald Reagan became president, it grew some more. Although it may surprise some people, while Reagan and George Bush were bashing the federal bureaucracy for twelve years, they increased it by three hundred thousand civilian positions. Even more surprising, perhaps, is that President Clinton has reduced federal civilian positions by two hundred thousand and former secretary Henry Cisneros cut HUD positions by 13 percent.

In his book *Federal Government and Urban Problems,* former HUD bureaucrat M. Carter McFarland muses, "Why so late?" Why did it take until 1965 for the federal government to create HUD? "By any realistic standard, the establishment of a cabinet department to represent urban interests was late in coming."

The delay may have resulted in part because until the postwar era, housing markets in U.S. cities included a variety of low-cost options. Former *New York Daily News* columnist Pete Hamill, throughout his book *A Drinking Life,* describes the housing available in New York City before urban renewal began. Not all the housing was pretty, and some could be a tight fit, but the options included walk-ups, apartments over stores, triplexes, duplexes, single-family houses, apartments over garages, flats in back, boardinghouses, tenements, and row houses.

Destroying the Village to Save It

Cities had low-cost, affordable housing before the federal government invented it. Tenements, low-rent hotels, flophouses, what are

How the Government Killed
Affordable Housing

now called single-room occupancy apartments (SROs)—all served people with low incomes, often immigrants, seeking to make it in the city. And many of them did make it, in part because they found what they needed in the urban housing market. Though much of this housing fell short of today's standards and much of it was filled beyond safe capacity, people were never separated from the weave of urban life by contrived housing arrangements. They found shelter they could afford while they worked to afford bigger or better shelter. They both improved their housing and made their living by working. They did not think to look to the federal government.

Efficient, low-income housing techniques grew organically in cities. The simplest was for people to live where they worked, literally. At the turn of the century it was common for people to live above the shops on a commercial street. A builder or developer could add a story or two of apartments above a commercial establishment, increasing value at little extra cost. The tenants attracted to these apartments generally had jobs, albeit often low-wage jobs. They worked in the establishments below them or nearby on the street. Sometimes the shop owners themselves lived above the shops. As people earned more money, they moved a block or two away from the street where they worked, perhaps even buying a house, freeing the lower-cost housing for others.

Low-cost housing in cities was not restricted to rental properties. In Milwaukee, German and Polish immigrants with peasant backgrounds, usually working at low-wage industrial jobs, placed an extremely high value on home ownership. They felt that land ownership and home ownership would save them from returning to the serfdom they had escaped in their homelands. To the Polish immigrants, home ownership was not the result of success, but a means to success. Through self-denial and inventiveness, they found ways to own their own homes. One of their creations was known as the "Polish flat."

The Polish flat was a modest, three- or four-room cottage built with the first money these immigrants could save in their new land.

As the mortgage was paid off, the owner of the cottage typically would raise it on posts four or five feet high in order to construct a semibasement living space, with a separate entrance, below. Sometimes this space was occupied by newly arrived, income-earning members of the owner's family or extended family; sometimes it was let to boarders. As soon as additional income allowed, the timber beams of the basement were replaced with brick walls. Rooms were added to the upper floor. Sometimes cottages were lifted off their foundations and rolled through the neighborhood to be joined to the homes of their kin. You could tell the Polish families that had made it in Milwaukee—they no longer used the basement for income and had converted the duplex to a single-family unit.

Turn-of-the-century Milwaukee featured wards filled with Polish flats. Specifically designed both to accommodate and to accelerate the economic improvement of the family, Polish flats were human values reflected in architecture and testified to the hard work, practicality, and optimism of their inhabitants.

Another urban housing form common in Milwaukee was the two-story, two-family duplex, the prevalent style in German neighborhoods. German immigration to Milwaukee began in the middle of the nineteenth century, a few decades earlier than Polish immigration. Unlike the mostly rural Polish peasants who fled repression to create a better life, many German immigrants had wealth and brought with them skills more marketable in cities.

The arriving Germans recognized the need for rental units in a booming city and, as did their Polish counterparts, thought it made sense to earn income from their dwellings. The German artisans and skilled laborers, however, didn't take an incremental approach to building and owning their own homes. The two-flat duplex—often enhanced with leaded-glass windows, finely handcrafted woodwork, and other amenities—filled the needs of many German families.

In Milwaukee and other big cities, this is how the housing market worked. People shaped it according to their abilities and needs.

How the Government Killed
Affordable Housing

Atlanta and Houston generated the one-story shotgun house, Chicago the brick bungalow, and Philadelphia filled half its area with two-flat townhouses.

There were sometimes gaps in the urban housing market. The free-market system is not and cannot be perfect. Sometimes markets take a while to work. The incredibly rapid urbanization of the United States during the industrial revolution caused the gears of the housing market to grind and chafe painfully in an effort to keep up, particularly in the major destination city of immigrants, New York. Nearly a half million immigrants arrived in New York City in 1888 alone. Sixteen million arrived through Ellis Island between 1892 and 1920.

In 1890, muckraking journalist Jacob Riis produced *How the Other Half Lives,* a book about unhealthy living conditions in some New York tenements. Conditions were similar, if not quite so notorious, in other big cities. Riis's book focused public attention on real public-health problems, resulting in valuable improvements in services, such as immunization programs and better water, sewer, and sanitation efforts. But a detrimental consequence of the book was the attachment of a stigma to such urban housing forms as New York City's tenements and Boston's triplexes. Housing reformers spread the notion of a housing shortage, claiming that the market had failed. Yet from the Civil War until the Great Depression, "the private housing market generated a cornucopia of housing forms to accommodate those of modest means." The Boston triple-decker houses vilified by reformers, for example, were often owner occupied.

At first New York, Chicago, and other cities paid for public housing themselves through local housing authorities. Cities built, or helped build, only what they could afford, and thus they built to human scale. In 1920 in Milwaukee, money was appropriated to assist in cooperative home building. Typical pre–World War II public housing in Milwaukee consisted of two- or three-story apartment buildings. These buildings had an institutional look, with small concrete stoops, metal window frames, and no real porches. Unlike the federally funded high-rise housing built later, many of these earlier buildings are still in service and attractive to tenants.

While cities spent money hoping to fill the perceived housing gap, state and federal governments worked to widen it. Bureaucrats and planners began to damn the very urban neighborhoods that were playing such a valuable role in assimilating immigrants and low-income citizens. Of the poor but marvelously functional and upwardly mobile Polish neighborhoods of Milwaukee, one state health official noted:

> *The 12th and 14th wards are more than any others the regions of the modern cave dwellers. . . .*
>
> *. . . The basements are occupied from choice and long fixed habit, as well as, in some cases, to reduce the cost of living. In many cases well-to-do owners of the property are found living in the basement when the first floor rooms are vacant. The only excuse for such living is ignorance. . . . In fact, the basement has a musty, sour, human smell that they like.*

Such frightening prejudice against immigrants and people living in poverty fueled many state and federal improvement programs for cities. The exalted ideals of reformers bumped into and crushed the humble dreams—and houses—of the immigrants.

Neighborhoods did struggle with problems of sanitation and public health, but these problems had less to do with the type or density of buildings than with the primitive state of medical and municipal services. Small lots and multifamily units saved space and made housing more affordable. University of Wisconsin–Milwaukee researchers Judith T. Kenny and Thomas C. Hubka argue that "crowded houses and lots did exist as a mechanism for the unskilled laborer's family to finance their basic needs."

It is a legitimate role for government to protect public health, provide clean water, and ensure safe buildings. These problems are not, however, inherent to dense housing patterns or particular housing

How the Government Killed
Affordable Housing

styles. Some of today's most desirable urban neighborhoods are among the most densely populated. Washington, D.C.'s Georgetown, New York's Greenwich Village, and Boston's North End all feature housing styles that government tried to eliminate.

In his first speech as mayor of Milwaukee in 1916, Dan Hoan said, "Congestion of the population is a serious problem confronting our community. This can be overcome only by a spreading out of the population."

To spread people out, cities began putting limitations on lot coverage. This policy backfired in Milwaukee and elsewhere, as Kenny and Hubka point out:

Lot coverage restrictions gradually eliminated new construction of the rear house and the Polish Flat and contributed to the long term decentralization of the population. As a consequence, home ownership and the stability and status associated with it would be more difficult to acquire.

The government war on dense neighborhoods ignored their value. Town planner Leopold Kohr argues that "slums contain amenities offered by none of the resettlements the authorities have put in their place." He cites their location and the closely packed ingredients of a self-sufficient neighborhood as their primary amenities: "These are precisely the amenities which city planners and rehabilitators—their instincts dulled by scientific bias—are forever tempted to take away."

To destroy dense neighborhoods, cities also began to wield the power of zoning. In 1930 the Hoover administration developed a model zoning ordinance that emphasized separated uses; that is, it physically separated houses from commercial and industrial activity. The Hoover model ordinance helped spread single-use zoning in cities nationwide.

Separate-use zoning responded to legitimate health concerns raised by people's living near noxious factories, stockyards, and rendering plants. The nineteenth-century industrial revolution changed cities by adding mass production with attendant pollution to their traditional functions as markets and cultural centers. European cities most often chose to exile industry to the edge. The industrial environs outside Paris, the Midlands well north of London, Nowa Huta outside Kraków—all are separate industrial concentrations that enable the beauty and value of the traditional city to be preserved.

In the United States, separate-use zoning was applied more comprehensively. Instead of merely separating the city from the noxious residue of mass production, we have separated housing from every other human activity. The result is the familiar pattern we see today in edge-city suburbs—commercial offices in one parking pod, commercial retail in another, light industrial in another, and housing on cul-de-sacs, completely isolated from everything. Housing subdivisions consequently have no corner stores and nothing much else within walking distance, except more housing.

Dead-End Housing

Today's suburban housing pattern started with the romantic and heavenly ideals of the cemetery movement of the mid-nineteenth century. In the United States, until 1840, graveyards and burial plots were small and close together. The graveyard of New York City's Trinity Church, which Wall Street stockbrokers visit when they need to put their losses in proper perspective, is an example. The Mount Auburn cemetery in Cambridge, Massachusetts, described by Garry Wills in *Lincoln at Gettysburg,* however, was created as a necropolis, a "city of the dead," on a hill. With curved streets, landscaped lawns, and shade trees, Mount Auburn resembles the basic suburban subdivision of today. Its idealized appearance was meant to represent heaven on earth, and it was an absolute sensation, attracting not only mourners, but also Bostonians taking post-church buggy rides and tourists from across the United States.

How the Government Killed
Affordable Housing

The Mount Auburn style spread. Mount Greenwood in Chicago, Forest Home in Milwaukee, Forest Lawn in Los Angeles, and thousands more cemeteries were named after various combinations of mountains, forests, lawns, and hills and represented the ideal metropolis—pastoral and perfect.

Meanwhile, the advent of commuter trains began to allow people to commute conveniently into cities from farther away. The wealthy citizens of cities created garden subdivisions—New Yorkers created Scarsdale, Philadelphians the Mainline, and Chicagoans the North Shore. The first garden subdivision, Llewellyn Park, was built in West Orange, New Jersey, in 1853. A ferry ride and a train ride from Manhattan, Llewellyn Park had no stores, shops, or factories, only mansions that spread along curving roads among trees and lawns, much like Mount Auburn cemetery.

Although only rich people could afford the commuting costs, with mass production of the automobile, garden subdivisions became affordable for the middle class. In fact, Herbert Hoover's model code and the resulting single-use zoning codes adopted across the country made the garden subdivision almost the only choice for anyone wanting to build a home. Nearly overnight, with the widespread adoption of these codes, the corner store with living space overhead ceased to be built in the United States. Main Street as we know it, with its mixed uses and pedestrian orientation, became a historical rather than contemporary form.

Separated, single-use zoning hurts U.S. cities. The code promoted by the federal government diminishes diversity and proximity, the key physical advantages of cities.

French architect Leon Krier has compared the city to a cake. The ingredients of a cake, if mixed and baked properly, produce a tasty treat. But those same ingredients—eggs, flour, sugar, butter, and water—are not very appealing if considered separately and, if consumed separately, are not very tasty. In the same way, housing, retail stores, hotels, and office buildings—each separated and surrounded by its own parking lot—are less attractive than the properly assembled city.

Hoover isn't entirely to blame, of course. Some cities were moving toward separate-use zoning on their own. Hoover simply reinforced and accelerated the process. The federal government took a decent idea—separating noxious industrial uses from other uses—and extended it too far, so far that the urban form has become nearly illegal.

Warehousing the Poor

In 1937, as part of the New Deal, Congress passed a public-housing law creating the United States Housing Authority. It wasn't a bad law. During the Great Depression, federal loans helped cities build and manage new housing for their impoverished citizens. This was a unique time, when dust-bowl migration to cities created a need for shelter, and home-construction work helped end the depression. Cities and local housing groups used federal tools to construct housing to meet local conditions. Most of it was two-story and three-story construction, widely scattered in large and small communities. Primarily working middle-class and upwardly mobile tenants lived in buildings of monotonous design, but "this type of housing with this type of tenant presented no great problems and helped many."

Early public housing simply shadowed the natural housing market, filling in gaps in supply where incomes and demand dictated. Shortly before and after the war, for instance, public housing helped house war workers and military personnel. It supplemented a housing market that had been disrupted first by the depression and then by war.

By 1950 federal public housing—intended to be a temporary program during a time of economic distress—had outlived its usefulness. Its clients were disappearing. Wage earners had less need for a temporary place to stay. The federal housing bureaucracy, small as it was, could have been easily dismantled. Instead, aided by Congress, it looked for, and found, a new problem, a new clientele, thus ensuring its perpetuation.

The midcentury migration of poor African Americans to big cities was regarded by housing bureaucrats as a cause. Before the gears of

How the Government Killed
Affordable Housing

the urban housing markets could click into place, before dislocated and disadvantaged African Americans had a chance to settle and create their own housing strategies as had immigrant groups before them, the federal government followed the utopian vision of Swiss planner Le Corbusier and built high-rises separated from the urban fabric by lawns and parking lots.

HUD bureaucrat McFarland, in retrospect, recognizes these high-rises as a blunder. He explains that racism and "bitter local resistance" put limits on where public housing could be built. "Where sites could be found," he says, "the land was expensive. Expensive land made high-rise construction an economic necessity."

The government's approach resulted in such infamous projects as Pruit-Igoe in St. Louis, where twelve thousand African Americans with incomes at or below poverty level were warehoused in a high-rise apartment complex and expected to create a community. They didn't. Pruit-Igoe, the Robert Taylor homes in Chicago, and scores of similar projects were complete disasters.

I visited the Robert Taylor homes in 1991 along with Captain Arthur Jones, now Milwaukee's police chief. Our tour was led by Hosea Crossley, commander of the Chicago Housing Authority (CHA) police. We viewed efforts that had been made to improve Taylor homes, including a building that was sealed to eliminate drug dealers, and day-care service and police substation in one of the high-rises. In the substation I noticed seven-foot-high shields propped against one wall."What are the shields for?" I asked Hosea.

"Snipers," he replied. "We use them to get to our squad cars when they're shooting at us."

IN THE 1950s, 1960s, and 1970s urban renewal captured the imaginations of planners and federal policy makers. Urban renewal meant the federal government paid to tear down neighborhoods. Acres and acres of urban land were cleared of so-called blight. Between 1950 and

1990, almost two-thirds of the population of St Louis was removed. The riverfront district, bigger than New Orleans's French Quarter and potentially as beautiful, was completely demolished. Gaslight Square, a once popular tourist attraction for jazz fans, was flattened. In Milwaukee, the Hotels Antlers, Randolph, and Plankinton, old railroad hotels seeking to survive in the age of beltways and suburbs by letting rooms at low cost, were razed using federal subsidies. Examples abound of famous neighborhoods lost to urban renewal. In *The Living City,* Roberta Brandes Gratz discusses the planned destruction in the 1950s and 1960s of Coney Island, where "more money per square foot has been spent . . . to destroy a community than anywhere else."

From coast to coast U.S. cities used federal urban-renewal grants and, later, Urban Development Action grants (UDAG) to eliminate the blight of low-cost hotels and apartments. Removing blight really meant putting people without means on the streets and onto government dependence. By tearing down low-cost housing, the government forced private housing providers out of the market, made housing less affordable, and created both homelessness and a permanent public-housing clientele.

Journalist Pete Hamill rented an eight-dollar-a-month, one-room apartment in New York City after the war. Even in today's inflated dollars, that rent would be low, about one hundred dollars. This kind of opportunity was available in U.S. cities before urban renewal removed blight.

After much of the low-cost housing had been destroyed, the federal government realized the need for such housing and began a single-room occupancy, or SRO, program to increase the supply of one-person dwellings. For nearly two hundred years the market had produced low-cost housing in a variety of forms, shapes, and sizes. Now the only low-cost housing is produced by the government and not, considering tax subsidies, at low cost. This situation brings to mind President Reagan's description of federal economic policy: "If it moves, tax it; if it's still moving, regulate it; if it stops moving, sub-

How the Government Killed
Affordable Housing

sidize it." Having created a problem, the federal government, through HUD, began to look for a solution.

Less than a million public-housing units were created between 1937 and the formation of HUD in 1965. In 1968, Richard Nixon took office and appointed George Romney secretary of HUD. Romney was viewed as a pragmatic, nonideological Republican who could get things done. Like other automobile executives drafted into government service, Romney wanted to get product out the door. This approach worked well when auto executive Henry Kaiser built Liberty ships and B-24s during World War II—we won. It didn't work so well when Robert McNamara engineered the United States' most expensive and embarrassing defeat, Vietnam.

Romney kicked public housing into high gear. In 1970 alone, four hundred thousand public-housing units were created. They were often poorly constructed, poorly managed, and the focal point for exploitation and scandal by unscrupulous developers. Hundreds of real estate dealers, mortgage bankers, and federal employees were indicted and convicted under Romney for public-housing scams and kickbacks.

What is wrong with federally funded public housing other than poor targeting, poor design, poor management, and scandal? Just one thing: it's not needed.

Housing advocates mistakenly focus on production. The United States does not have a housing shortage. It has a distorted housing market. The federal government has made it easy for lenders to redline low-income housing in our city neighborhoods. By focusing on below-market public housing in those neighborhoods, the federal government smothers market mechanisms that would attract private-sector investment. Irving Welfeld explains in *HUD Scandals*:

> *Unfortunately, we have made a fundamental error. We have combined the production and assistance function. The main thrust of American housing policy has been to assist poor people by supplying them with new housing.*

The catchword, at present, is "affordable housing.". . . If the poor cannot afford food, we earmark assistance and give them food stamps. We don't create farms that grow only "affordable food" or build "affordable food" supermarkets where only the poor can shop.

Subsidizing Sprawl

Unlike most government inventions, the Federal Housing Authority (FHA) was efficient and effective from the moment it was established by President Franklin Roosevelt. Its goal was to create jobs through housing construction, and it did. The FHA was one of the New Deal's most respected entities.

Although intended to fill a temporary gap in the housing market caused by the Great Depression, when the depression ended, the FHA didn't. Over the next forty years, the FHA insured almost $200 billion in mortgage loans. These loans, rather than being used for duplexes, apartments, condominiums, or other urban forms, were used for detached, single-family, new construction. The FHA effectively went about the business of subsidizing the suburbanization of the United States. It diverted capital from the urban housing market by focusing almost exclusively on new, single-family homes in the suburbs.

For most of its existence, the FHA hasn't been necessary. Mortgage insurance has been widely available in the private market since the mid-1950s. Mortgage Guarantee Insurance Corporation and Fleet Mortgage are two large mortgage-insurance companies that operate out of Milwaukee. Many others are headquartered throughout the United States. These companies employ thousands of people but have to compete every day with the federal government.

Lenders who use it find it hard not to like the FHA subsidy. Not surprisingly, elected officials like what the voters seem to like. FHA bureaucrats are proud of its success. McFarland counts as one of the FHA's successes the "creation of a mass-production home building industry" that no longer had to depend on the "single,

How the Government Killed
Affordable Housing

customized transaction." He is proud that the FHA could make it "possible for builders to plan and construct large subdivisions without identifying the particular purchasers in advance. This made possible speculative, relatively large-scale home-building ventures." The buyers came from existing neighborhoods that had no FHA program to capitalize their rehabilitation needs. The buyers were also overwhelmingly white. Racial covenants were encouraged to protect value. As late as 1960, "not one of Levittown's [N.Y.] 82,000 residents was black." For the FHA, creditworthiness was synonymous with whiteness. The Kerner Commission report notes that until 1949, the FHA's official policy was not to insure any nonsegregated housing; it wasn't until thirteen years later, in 1962, that an executive order made the agency require nondiscrimination pledges from loan applicants. Looking back on the early days of the FHA, Milwaukee realtor Beechie Brooks commented, "In some ways the federal government was a worse redliner than any bank."

HUD to the Rescue?

The Johnson administration recognized that at best, housing programs were helping middle-class families leave town and at worst, they were hurting poor families. Rather than end the programs, Johnson created HUD and brought the FHA under its wing. Among the very first programs begun under the new arrangement were the home-ownership and rental subsidy programs. Despite their proper focus, existing housing, Welfeld refers to these programs as a "headlong rush to the cliff." In a few short years they were awash in red ink and scandal. They worked on paper only by overestimating client incomes and underestimating expenses. They could not work in real life. The home-ownership program gave more mortgage money to its poor clients than they could possibly absorb. Political obsession with home ownership resulted in people being swindled into buying overpriced, overmortgaged, low-quality homes. In

1973, President Nixon ordered HUD secretary Jim Lynn to stop FHA-subsidized housing programs. Subsequent HUD efforts have not been much more successful.

Sheldon Lubar, Milwaukee business executive and HUD assistant secretary of housing production and mortgage credit under Presidents Nixon and Ford, described the situation this way:

The expansion of FHA to existing housing killed Detroit. Real estate speculators scared out the whites for $10,000 and sold the houses to blacks for $18,000 using FHA mortgages. There was no incentive to check credit because the loans were guaranteed. The abandonment of actuarily sound mortgage insurance led to the destruction of vast neighborhoods of the central city.

Today HUD administers dozens of programs, among them

- Homeless Assistance Grants
- Emergency Food and Shelter
- Education for Homeless Children and Youth
- PATH Formula Grants (for homeless people)
- Community Development Block Grants
- HOME Investment Partnership
- Public Housing Operating Subsidies
- Public Housing Modernization
- Severely Distressed Public Housing
- Elderly/Disabled Housing
- Loan Guarantees
- Section 8 Renewals
- Preservation
  and more . . .

How the Government Killed Affordable Housing

Each program adds between $40 million and $4.6 billion to the national debt each year, and each is intended to solve a specific problem, usually created by government. HUD has eleven thousand federal permanent, full-time employees. That's more than one hundred federal workers for every central city in the United States.

HUD can't seem to decide who its clients are and what to do for them. Congress hasn't helped. Over the years it has directed housing programs to sprint one way, stop, turn around, and sprint the other way. Until 1949 low- and middle-income wage earners were public-housing clients. For the next twenty-five years policy decisions wavered back and forth, but gradually excluded all wage earners except those with the lowest incomes. In the mid-1970s Congress "tried to turn the clock back to the good old days" and appeal to a broader range of incomes. Not surprisingly, it was too late to induce "role-model" families to live in what had become shabby, crime-ridden projects. In the 1980s the tide turned back to providing services only for people with the very lowest incomes.

Money from an agency with no clear direction or mission distorts natural urban markets. Red tape and inefficiency make it harder for cities to address their own problems. In Milwaukee, for example, we wanted to keep drug addicts away from elderly public-housing residents. HUD wouldn't let us.

Your Grandma Lives with Drug Addicts

Many elderly people seem able to live relatively peacefully in the high-rise apartments so inappropriate for low-income family living. Local housing authorities began to convert failed family housing high-rises to elderly housing. In Milwaukee, these changes were working well. Then HUD came along in the 1970s and said that local housing authorities couldn't segregate the elderly population. The agency's rules required that elderly people live with people with disabilities.

The word *disabled* tends to raise positive, or at least sympathetic, associations in the public mind. People are apt to picture a person in a wheelchair, with multiple sclerosis or some other physical challenge, when they hear the phrase "people with disabilities." Under HUD's rules, however, *disabled* included people with drug or alcohol addictions and often these people had criminal records.

Not only did HUD require housing drug addicts and criminals in the same buildings with elderly people, but it also required housing them on the same floors. To avoid discrimination against the "disabled," not even a single floor could be set aside for senior citizens to live apart from the criminals, drug addicts, and alcohol abusers. A conspiracy theorist might think this was a calculated attempt to drive law-abiding citizens out of federally subsidized housing in order to turn it into an extension of the crowded federal prison system.

As a state senator in 1987, I visited a high-rise housing unit on Twenty-fourth and Cherry Streets on the west side of Milwaukee. The elderly residents cried as they pleaded with me to help get the drug addicts and criminals off their floors. They were being abused, intimidated, and attacked. It was a grim existence for people who wanted to enjoy their golden years in peace.

The Milwaukee Housing Authority was told by its lawyers that nothing could be done, which was technically true. To his credit, the head of the Department of City Development at the time, William Drew, had complained about the law and tried to change it. But it was the law, and according to HUD, that was that.

For the four years before I became mayor in 1988, only a handful of elderly residents applied to be in public housing. Elderly people were not asking for public housing because they didn't want to get hurt. Where they were going, no one was sure. Some certainly found other accommodations where they could choose safe company, but other probably did not.

Every time we asked the Reagan and Bush administrations to change the law, regional administrators came to my office to listen at-

How the Government Killed
Affordable Housing

tentively. Then they told me there was nothing they could do. They suggested we deal with the security problems on a case-by-case basis.

I called Congressman Gerald Kleczka, whose district includes the south side of Milwaukee. I told him that I wanted the law changed and that it was important. I asked him to pass a law that would allow elderly public-housing residents to live not only on separate floors, but in separate buildings.

"Do you want me to introduce this just so you can say something is being tried," asked Kleczka, "or do you really want this to pass?"

"Jerry, I want it to pass."

"I'll try," he said. At the time the Democrats still controlled Congress and Kleczka was a member of the Ways and Means Committee. He went to bat for us. With the HUD bureaucrats and advocacy-group extremists fighting him the whole way, Jerry got the bill passed and signed by President Bush in the spring of 1992.

There was much rejoicing. We thought we had made it. We contacted members of the Bush administration to see when we could start keeping our seniors safe and were told that they couldn't write the new rules required by law before the fall election. I realized that the bureaucracy was not about to change simply because the law required it.

That fall Bush lost. Maybe the delay in addressing the housing legislation wasn't the one big issue that caused his defeat, but it sure didn't help him among the elderly voters at Twenty-fourth and Cherry in Milwaukee.

Hopes rose when Bill Clinton assumed the presidency, but it turned out that HUD remained averse to change with Clinton in power also. HUD bureaucrats dragged their feet as long as possible. The new rules were delayed by Roberta Achtenberg, an assistant secretary of HUD and former San Francisco county commissioner who had an affinity for criminal rights. She didn't understand what we were trying to accomplish. Finally, after continued pressure from Kleczka and Wisconsin senators Herb Kohl and Russ Feingold, the Clinton administration changed the rules—thirteen months after Clinton was sworn in.

Now we have a waiting list of over four hundred senior citizens for Milwaukee's public housing. Our elderly public-housing clients have seven buildings to themselves where they are safe.

But the elderly residents in public housing aren't the only people who need to be safe. By working with landlords, cities can help improve safety in private residential property, too.

Landlord Training Program

When it comes to public image, landlords are right next to politicians and used-car dealers. Yet private landlords, not the government, provide most of the low-cost housing in the United States. Much of this housing is in pretty good shape. Some is not.

That's where building-code enforcement has traditionally stepped in. "Get the bad apples!" is the cry of building inspectors. And bad apples are there to get. Court-enforced penalties may be the only way to deal with genuine slumlords, but a hundred and fifty years of experience has taught Milwaukee building inspectors that people who own and manage residential property can be negligent, careless, and ultimately unsuccessful simply because they don't know what they are doing.

Inspectors were using up valuable time chasing the same code violators renting to the same bad tenants over and over again. Then deputy building inspector Marty Collins had the idea for the Landlord Training Program (LTP). In the LTP, building inspectors teach landlords how legally to screen against bad tenants—tenants who have a history of damaging property, engaging in criminal activity such as drug dealing, or not paying rent. They also teach that well-kept property attracts reliable tenants. The program provides tips to landlords on how more easily to comply with code requirements and, as important, it gives building inspectors an opportunity to learn from landlords.

When the LTP started, only a few landlords showed up. They liked it; word spread fast; and now more than 30 percent of Milwaukee's landlords have completed the program. Over 93 percent of those who have taken the course rated it excellent, and code violations among those trained are down substantially. Also in part as a result of the LTP, landlords are also helping the police reduce illegal drug use and crime related to drugs.

The Drug-Abatement Program

Drug dealers make bad long-term tenants. Sure, they pay cash for the first month's rent, and they might even pay for month number two, but before long they hold a rent party (that's when you spend the rent on having a party), tear the place apart, and move on to an apartment owned by someone else. The drug dealer relies on the new landlord not to ask for references or talk to the previous land-lord.

Traditionally, the police have attacked the illegal-drug trade by making a buy, getting an arrest warrant, and arresting the dealer. Although this process works, it is slow and cumbersome because it requires a high level of quality evidence to lead to a conviction.

Milwaukee's building inspectors, police, and neighborhood groups together devised the Drug Abatement Program (DAB). Lieutenant David Bruss, deputy building inspector Marty Collins, and dozens of neighborhood organizations and block clubs united to set it in motion.

DAB encourages landlords to evict immediately suspected drug sellers. Although the police investigate, arrest, and incarcerate when they can, the idea is to confront and remove drug dealing right away, even if this means passing up the opportunity to stage a big drug raid. Why? Because people, especially children, who live near the suspected drug house need quick relief from the threat to their lives and property.

As soon as drug activity is suspected, the landlord is informed and asked to evict. Police monitor the suspects if they move to another location in Milwaukee. Statistical review shows that drug sellers stop after being confronted. In over 85 percent of DAB cases, the police department finds "no further drug activity for a period of sixty days after commencement of the investigation of the complaint." The suspected drug dealers don't simply move to a new house in the city and start over. They know that the police have them on the watch list and that cooperating landlords have them on a list as well. Drug dealers are thus confronted informally, but swiftly and effectively. DAB is a local effort that adds value to Milwaukee.

How to Win the Housing War: Retreat

Reacting to a problem created in part by federally financed highway construction and urban-renewal programs, Congress passed the McKinney Act in 1986. Under this act, homeless people receive federal help from subsidized soup kitchens and shelters. The unintended consequence of this act, however, is even more homelessness.

Congress and Presidents Reagan, Bush, and now Clinton can appear compassionate by allocating relatively small amounts of money for shelters, soup kitchens, and food pantries as they continue to spend massive amounts to subsidize suburban housing and sprawl-inducing superhighways. The federal government is deep in debt from spending trillions to create the problem of homelessness. Rather than spending a relatively small amount that addresses only the worst symptoms of its own policies, the federal government should end the policies that fuel the problem. One logical starting place is reduction of mortgage subsidies, whether through Fanny Mae, the FHA, or the mortgage-interest deduction.

The principal effect of the mortgage-interest deduction has been to force capital into building larger and more expensive homes for fewer and fewer people. In 1994, income earners in the top 20 percent received $63 billion in housing subsidies; those in the bottom 20 percent received $18.7 billion, the middle 60 percent received $21.9 billion. The bigger and more expensive the home, the more valuable the tax write-off.

How the Government Killed
Affordable Housing

What the housing market really needs is for the federal government to keep its own finances under control so that low interest rates can benefit all people, regardless of their income or their housing choices.

To make this idea politically palatable, the current mortgage-interest deduction could be capped at the level of interest required to finance a half-million-dollar home. Over time, as housing prices increase, the deduction would have a decreasing impact on housing decisions.

The federal government should stop producing new public housing, but people already living in public housing should be allowed to stay as long as they follow the rules. Over time, the private market can produce low-cost housing much more efficiently than can the government. The federal government won't and probably can't finance public housing for everyone near the bottom end of the income scale. The presence of public housing, both through its buildings and through rent subsidies, distorts the low-cost housing market by chasing away private investors, raising rents, and reducing the amount of quality housing available for people who are poor but can't get public housing.

Local governments should reform their zoning practices. Low-cost housing, not subsidized by the federal government, could be created if cottages and apartments over stores were allowed. If there were no prohibition on combining commercial and residential uses on streets intended for commercial use, developers could build low-cost housing on top of commercial venues such as video stores, supermarkets, fast-food outlets, or drugstores. If zoning laws stop prohibiting developers from building multiple-use buildings, developers will respond, as they have in Japan, western Europe, and Canada as well as a few U.S. cities, such as Providence, Rhode Island, Charleston, South Carolina, and San Francisco.

As part of the 1989 savings-and-loan bailout, Community Reinvestment Act mandates require banks to show their commitment to serving minorities and low-income neighborhoods. Cities should not use this act to encourage banks to be charitable; rather, they should encourage banks to establish profitable and therefore sustainable operations.

As in other areas of human activity and commerce, cities have natural advantages in the housing market. Cities ought to have the highest-quality housing at the most reasonable cost. The natural value of cities, if allowed expression, could address a significant part of the housing needs and desires of people in the United States.

City-States

HISTORICALLY, cities have been havens and markets, the common destination for people seeking safety and prosperity, as well as for merchants seeking customers. Cities have benefited from the free movement of goods and people across political and geographic borders and in turn have bestowed benefits on their new and established citizens.

With their multiplicity of goods and large demands, their international monetary capabilities and communications infrastructure, their mixture of cultures and ideas within markets, their naturally convenient locations, and their comprehensive transportation systems that include air, water, rail, and highway facilities, cities are ideally suited to conduct trade and generate wealth. Yet most U.S. cities are not considered wealthy. Part of the explanation may lie in federal restrictions on trade and immigration.

In northern Europe in the sixteenth century, most cities along the Baltic and North Seas formed a free-trade pact known as the Hanseatic League. The city-states of Antwerp, Bremen, Bruges, Danzig, Göteborg, Königsberg, Kraków, Lübeck, Riga, Visby, and many others were enriched by world trade. Eventually, nation-states emerged. These larger entities taxed, regulated, and distorted commerce. As they assumed power, the nation-states conducted war. War cost money; to raise the money, they taxed trade. They suppressed the economic freedom of the cities with taxes, tariffs, and embargoes. Trade among Hanseatic cities soon diminished, as did their wealth.

THE WEALTH OF CITIES

Washington Post columnist Neal Peirce believes that in part through a renewed dedication to free world trade, the twenty-first century will bring the reemergence of cities and metropolitan regions as crucibles of economic progress, as "the city-state was always a more natural political and economic entity than the nation-state."

One city that still trades freely and may be a harbinger of things to come is Hong Kong. Although Hong Kong's success is tempered by its democratic deficiencies and its former status as a protectorate has meant that its government has been relieved of paying for many basic duties, such as defense, William Peterson, in his essay "Free Trade Is the Best Trading System," suggests that Hong Kong is a model worth emulating. Economist Milton Friedman agrees.

Peterson and Friedman note that Hong Kong has a population density fourteen times that of Japan and almost two hundred times that of the United States, but a very high standard of living; it operates with no tariffs and no government direction of economic activity; and its ratio of government spending to per capita income is among the lowest in the world. Some of Hong Kong's economic accomplishments are represented by the following statistics:

- It is the world's largest exporter of garments, toys, and games.
- It is the world's second busiest container port, measured by volume (next to Rotterdam).
- It is the world's third largest international banking and financial center.
- It is second only to Japan in per capita gross national product in Asia.
- It has the highest telephone density in Southeast Asia.
- It has the second highest vehicle density in the world, next to Monaco.

Hong Kong, the modern equivalent of a city-state, trades freely and enjoys the second highest standard of living in Asia, next to Japan.

City-States

From the nationalists of sixteenth-century Denmark and Prussia to Ross Perot in twentieth-century United States, opponents of free trade have failed to understand one fundamental economic principle. The process of free trade creates—not merely exchanges—wealth. As Adam Smith observed, trade is a voluntary exchange that benefits both parties. Party A may have widgets and need gizmos. Party B may have gizmos and need widgets. Under the laws of supply and demand, gizmos are more valuable to party A than are widgets, and widgets are more valuable to party B than are gizmos. The parties decide to trade a widget for a gizmo. Each party trades something of relatively less value for something of relatively greater value. After the trade, each party has more value than it had before. The total wealth of the two parties together surpasses their total wealth prior to the trade.

Governments often lose sight of the simple benefits of free trade and use trade as a weapon or political tool. They sometimes restrain the choices of their citizens by distorting the simple process of trade, portraying it as a zero-sum game that can somehow be won. This viewpoint results in (1) a tangled web of tariffs, quotas, boycotts, embargoes, and subsidies; (2) a parasitic trade bureaucracy whose job seems to be to destroy wealth-generating processes while sucking money out of the economy in the form of taxes; and (3) a poorer world.

Economist Henry George voiced these issues over a hundred years ago:

> *Protective tariffs are as much applications of force as are blockading squadrons, and their object is the same—to prevent trade. The difference between the two is that blockading squadrons are a means whereby nations seek to prevent the enemies from trading; protective tariffs are a means whereby nations attempt to prevent their own people from trading.*

Journalist and former World Bank consultant James Bovard views U.S. trade laws as based on the notion of economic war. Their purpose is to attempt "to prevent foreigners from dumping their products, bankrupting U.S. companies, and then taking over the market and vicitimizing American consumers." The flaw in this thinking is that this scenario is not likely to happen; foreign monopoly of U.S. markets is highly improbable. As Bovard puts it, "Our trade laws routinely inflate domestic prices against the one-in-a-million possibility that a foreign company could corner the market and raise prices."

Federal government has a legitimate role in trade, but it isn't to conduct economic war. International organizations of nations can facilitate commerce in cities—they can foster mutual, wealth-producing economic transactions—by aiding safe navigation, defending against piracy, and protecting patents and copyrights. At its founding, the United States was dedicated to free commerce within the nation and access to markets of the world. U.S. cities have benefited greatly from the consequent easy flow of commerce within the nation. The European Community, recognizing the benefits of a seamless economy, has based much of its organization on the U.S. Interstate Commerce clause.

U.S. cities also benefit from our defense of the world's trade routes, but they are hurt mightily by special-interest trade barriers that restrict their access to world markets. (As destinations that thrive on diversity, cities are also harmed, as I'll discuss later, by overly restrictive laws regarding the movement of people.) Government and special-interest interference in the market works against the natural advantages of cities. A key ingredient to making U.S. cities rich again is to reduce the federal government's interference with trade and immigration. If New York, Los Angeles, Seattle, New Orleans, Houston, Milwaukee, and Cleveland can import and export goods without interference, these cities and others will produce greater wealth for the United States.

Big Steel

Each spring, about fifty-five dockworkers move general cargo at the port of Milwaukee. They earn about eighteen dollars per hour unloading and loading ships, most of which carry steel from foreign nations. Steel enters Milwaukee as a raw material. Industrial engineers, foundry workers, forgers, toolmakers, and assemblers then turn it into machines that attract buyers from around the globe. From Harnischfeger mining shovels to Harley-Davidson motorcycles, products made in Milwaukee serve markets worldwide.

In February 1993, at the request of the U.S. steel industry, the U.S. Commerce Department brought charges of illegal dumping against almost every foreign manufacturer of steel. *Illegal dumping* is the term used by large U.S. steel manufacturers to describe what most people would call price competition. Germany, the United Kingdom, Italy, France, and Canada—all of them U.S. allies—were among the countries accused of conducting economic war on the United States.

Although the February dumping charges would not be acted on until July, when it was likely that heavy tariffs would be placed on foreign steel, the price of U.S. steel jumped immediately in anticipation of the closure of the U.S. market to competitors. Because any finding of dumping would be retroactive, steel shipments to Milwaukee from other countries were canceled. When spring arrived, instead of fifty-five dockworkers working at the port of Milwaukee, there were five. Nearly $2 million a year in dockworker wages was being lost to the Milwaukee economy. Forty-five dockworkers were put out of work in Toledo, Ohio, and substantial layoffs also hit the ports of New Orleans, Philadelphia, Long Beach, California, and Houston.

The effect on Milwaukee's metal-bending industry was even greater. Firms were suddenly paying inflated prices for scarce steel. Their products had to reflect increased costs and thus became less competitive on the world market, reducing industry jobs and profits.

"Steel prices skyrocketed, supply disappeared and worst of all for us the ships never came," protested Donald Baumgartner, chairman of Wisconsin Paper Machinery. Baumgartner uses the foreign ships that haul steel to Milwaukee's port to haul his container-manufacturing machines away. "U.S steel manufacturers and their pals in the Commerce Department forced us to ship machines out by truck and rail to the East Coast and it cost us a bundle."

The beneficiary of the higher taxes on foreign steel was the U.S. steel industry, especially Big Steel. Big Steel—Bethlehem, Inland, USX, and a few other companies—filed dumping charges even though U.S. steel producers already controlled 86 percent of the U.S. market. Steel executives claimed that foreigners gained the remaining 14 percent by artificially subsidizing steel. The tariffs were supposed to hurt foreign nations and help the United States. But the net effect of the fines was to raise steel prices to U.S. manufacturers, thereby increasing production costs and making it harder for U.S. manufacturers to compete in the world market.

U.S. trade policy is often dominated by special-interest groups such as Big Steel. Big Steel, most U.S. textile corporations, and some agricultural interests, such as the sugar lobby, love to talk about the virtues of free enterprise, but whine for subsidy and strict regulation of their competition when it comes to world trade. According to James Bovard, "Since 1983, the U.S. has brought more unfair-trade cases than any other country in the world. . . . It will investigate almost any import if so requested by a domestic industry."

Steel import quotas have resulted in displacement of U.S. companies from the high-grade steel market. Foreign steel companies realize they can only export so much to the United States so, naturally, they try to use their quota as efficiently as they can. They have conceded the low-grade steel market to U.S companies and export almost exclusively high-grade, high-margin steels. They have ratcheted up the quality and compete very favorably on the high end of the market. Without competition at the low end of the market, Big Steel can raise the price of low-grade steel. The federal government has thus driven down the quality of U.S.-made steel while driving up the price.

City-States

To disguise its self-interest, Big Steel tries to use a domestic security argument for subsidization. It claims that a rich domestic steel industry is necessary for national defense. In *Free to Choose*, Milton Friedman calls it inconceivable that free trade would render the U.S. steel industry incapable of producing that small fraction of steel necessary to meet our national defense needs. "Indeed," he says, "the need to meet foreign competition, rather than being sheltered behind governmental barriers, might very well produce a stronger and more efficient steel industry than we have today."

From the perspective of U.S. manufacturing cities, the federal government shouldn't complain when foreign steel producers lower prices. Instead, the federal government should shout, "Thank you! Thank you for lowering our cost of production of steel-based products. Thank you for taxing your citizens to make life less expensive for U.S. citizens. Thank you for challenging U.S. manufacturers to become more competitive."

The United States Conference of Mayors, the organization that is supposed to represent the interests of mayors and cities, takes positions each year on various issues brought to its attention by its members. Sometimes outside groups bring issues to the organization as well. It is well known that lobbyists for tobacco, the auto industry, beer, baseball, and steel hang out on Capitol Hill with the senators and congressmen. These same lobbyists hang out to a lesser extent at the USCM annual meeting.

In 1989, Big Steel tried to persuade the USCM to condemn steel dumping by the European Community and Japan. Richard Arrington, mayor of steel-producing Birmingham, Alabama, sponsored the resolution. It was about to pass as part of a bigger set of resolutions when I objected. The restrictions on steel imports would hurt the economies of Milwaukee and most USCM member cities, I argued, and the resolution should be defeated.

The chair of the meeting groaned and rolled his eyes, but I insisted on a separate vote. After Bud Clark, mayor of Portland, Oregon, and Federico Pena, mayor of Denver, agreed with me, something happened that rarely happens at USCM meetings—we had a full-blown debate on a policy issue! Mayor Arrington made his case for steel tariffs. Mayor Barnes of Gary, Indiana, joined him. Then Mayor Nao of Oxnard, California, asked why his taxpayers should subsidize the steel industry. Together we forged (so to speak) a majority. When the vote was taken, the Big Steel resolution lost by a large margin.

Some cities derive temporary economic advantage from artificial trade barriers. Gary and Birmingham, for instance, no doubt believe they benefit from the cozy relationship between Big Steel and Washington. Yet even these cities are more than likely hurt in the long run by such help.

An artificially protected economy is as bad for cities as drugs are for junkies. The recipients feel better for a while, but they soon become dependent and poisoned.

The economy of Gary, Indiana, has for more than a century depended on steel for its jobs and prosperity. Despite government protection of the industry, employment has steeply declined. The majority of the few steelworkers still employed live in affluent suburbs away from Gary's mills. Gary is located on the shores of Lake Michigan, but unlike Chicago, Milwaukee, Muskegon (Michigan), and most other cities on the lake, Gary's lakefront is industrial. Steel mills, mostly closed, dominate what could be a beautiful asset. Other lake cities prosper, while Gary hangs on to its hope for steel.

Pittsburgh, Pennsylvania, in contrast, has managed to wean itself more gracefully from the federal government's economic narcotic. It was difficult at first. When Pittsburgh's steel industry foundered in the early 1980s, the city discovered that it was not only unproductive, but dirty. Rather than perpetuate its dependency on steel, Pittsburgh entered a recovery program. By fostering its natural assets, Pittsburgh has become a beautiful and thriving city. This year it was named one of the fifteen most livable cities in the United States. A diversified economy featuring medical technology and

City-States

other high-tech sectors are carrying a stronger Pittsburgh into the twenty-first century.

Willie Wonka Would Weep

Ambrosia Chocolate in Milwaukee makes confectioners' chocolate and sells it to bakeries and other users of chocolate. The company does not make its own candy. To make candy, Ambrosia would have to buy U.S. sugar. Because of government trade protection, U.S. sugar is priced at about twice the world-market price. In *The Fair Trade Fraud,* Bovard notes that "for almost the entire history of the United States, American sugar prices have been held at double, triple, or quadruple the world sugar price."

When Ambrosia needed a new plant a few years ago, it considered moving to Canada because in Canada retail candy production made sense. Under the Canadian Free Trade Law, a plant in Canada could buy sugar at the lowest world-market price. With the U.S./Canadian Free Trade Act (now part of NAFTA), Ambrosia thought it could avoid U.S. sugar tariffs and quotas if it produced candy in Canada. The Canadian option did not pan out, however. The U.S. sugar lobby is so strong that it retained protection in the U.S.–Canada pact and in NAFTA, eliminating Canadian production as an option for U.S. manufacturers. Ambrosia continues to restrict its production to baker's chocolate. The real tragedy of this situation is that low-wage sugar-plantation jobs are protected at the expense of high-wage candy-making jobs in U.S. cities.

U.S. sugar-cane producers import labor from Jamaica and the Dominican Republic to work in fenced sugar-cane compounds in Florida. Through a loophole in the law, they pay grossly subminimum wages. They keep their workers locked up so that no one can escape and illegally enjoy the human rights and dignity afforded U.S. citizens. According to Bovard, from 1980 to 1990 these operations cost U.S. consumers and taxpayers over $2 million for each sugar grower.

To retain their welfare system, the sugar conglomerates lobby Congress to prop them up by prohibiting importation of sugar into the United States. The net effect of this action is that the U.S. government exports high-wage candy-manufacturing jobs overseas and imports exploited, low-wage, temporary, fenced laborers.

The Swiss government places no tariffs on sugar because the Swiss know they can sell high-quality candy all over the world. There are virtually no raw materials in Switzerland. In a strange way, the Swiss are blessed by a paucity of resources because they've learned how to make high-quality, value-added products. They sell their candy worldwide at good prices. They sell expensive watches even though they have to import all their metal. The Swiss have no tariffs or quotas on raw materials. Workers in Switzerland are paid well. Unemployment and poverty are almost unknown.

"The success of the United States," says Milton Friedman, "is often attributed to its generous natural resources and wide open spaces. They certainly played a part—but then, if they were crucial, what explains the success of nineteenth-century Great Britain and Japan or twentieth-century Hong Kong?" Or, for that, matter, what explains the failure of the country most endowed with natural resources—the Soviet Union?

The United States hasn't learned from Switzerland or the United Kingdom or Hong Kong. Instead, the U.S. government has slapped a huge quota on sugar. The sugar industry is a dirty little secret in the U.S. trade embargo on Cuba. No sugar at all is allowed into the United States from Cuba. The embargo isn't in place simply because Cuba is Communist. After all, we trade with Communist Vietnam, with whom we were at war less than twenty-five years ago, and with Communist China, a country with a shameful human-rights record. Many people attribute U.S. restrictions on trade with Cuba to the political impact of Cuban exiles. The Cuban American population does have an impact, but so do the armies of congressional lobbyists for Archer Daniels Midland, C&H, and Domino. These corporations have successfully squelched competition by befriending powers in

City-States

Washington such as Jesse Helms, Newt Gingrich, Bob Dole, Richard Gephardt, and Bill Clinton.

While we prop up rural Florida sugar plantations that use imported migrant labor, we repress high-wage manufacturing in U.S. cities. Meanwhile, the Swiss manufacture Toblerone candy and earn good wages. English workers make Cadbury. If you travel to the airports of the world, you rarely see U.S. candy being sold, but you do see Toblerone and Cadbury. We can't compete because the U.S. sugar lobby enjoys the protection of the federal government.

Steel. Sugar. Special interests, pursuing their own agendas at the expense of U.S. cities and the broader economic vitality of the nation. Yet a third group is also working counter to the economic health of U.S. cities—the shipping interests.

Davy Jones's Locker

In 1921, U.S shipping interests successfully lobbied the federal government to adopt a body of laws called the Jones Act. The Jones Act, among other things, restricts cabotage, the practice of coastal trading among the cities of a single country. The word *cabotage* comes from the Italian sailor and explorer John Cabot who, in the service of England in the late fifteenth century, explored the New World. His voyages were not well financed, so he supported himself and his sailors by carrying cargo from port city to port city.

Some U.S. shipowners didn't like this practice. Ships from France, Italy, the United Kingdom, Japan, Canada—all allies of the United States—are now strictly prohibited from carrying cargo or passengers between U.S. ports. It is illegal for a Canadian ship to carry a Harnischfeger crane from Milwaukee to Detroit. It is illegal for a British ship to carry newsprint from Seattle to Honolulu, or pineapples from Honolulu to Seattle.

U.S. shipbuilders got into the act, too. The Jones Act prohibits any ship that was manufactured anywhere else in the world, or is owned or ever was owned anywhere else in the world, from trading between two ports in the inland waterways of the United States, including

THE WEALTH OF CITIES

the Great Lakes and the shipping channels along the Atlantic and Pacific coasts, or to and from U.S. territories such as Guam and Puerto Rico. U.S. shipping interests feel entitled by their political involvement in federal elections to monopolize all waterborne trade between U.S. port cities.

Anticabotage policies are common, but the U.S. rules are among the world's most restrictive. The impact on U.S. seaports is costly. The impact on Great Lakes ports is devastating.

Today's largest ships are already prevented from getting to Milwaukee because they cannot physically get around Niagara Falls via the Welland Canal between Lake Ontario and Lake Erie. Only relatively small ships, about 40 to 45 percent of oceangoing ships, can use Great Lakes ports west of Niagara. With their limited cargo-carrying capacity, not many of these smaller ships can afford the long trip through the Great Lakes without cabotage. If a Dutch or Korean vessel could haul profitable cargo from Chicago to Milwaukee to Detroit, it would be more likely to enter the Great Lakes seaway. U.S. ships on the lakes would not suffer from this competition, as the only U.S. ships on the Great Lakes are too big to leave them. These ships haul iron ore, salt, sand, and coal; the smaller foreign ships would be unable to capture much, if any, of the bulk-product market.

Shipping along the East Coast has also been damaged by the Jones Act. Rob Quartel, president of the Jones Act Reform Coalition, asks "If the Jones Act is the god-send its beneficiaries say—if it provides jobs, protects seamen, supports a vast and mighty fleet, serves as a bulwark of America's defenses, and underpins the nation's ship-building industry—then where are the ships?" At the end of World War II, the U.S merchant marine consisted of more than five thousand ships. Now, reports Quartel, "only 50 ancient ships sail the Great Lakes, and not one coastal freighter serves the East Coast of the United States."

The Jones Act is just one federal subsidy for the U.S shipping industry. In the mid-1930s the United States recognized that world war threatened. To bolster the country's commercial and military readiness and to boost the depression-ravaged maritime economy, Congress passed the Merchant Marine Act of 1936.

This act effectively took away the competitive balance between shipyard and shipowner, shipowner and crew. It heavily subsidized U.S. shipbuilding, crews, and transport with the goal of quickly gearing up maritime capability while avoiding labor dissension. As the European war approached, demand for U.S. products increased, and once war began, demand skyrocketed, creating a huge need for U.S. merchant ships. Furthermore, U.S transport was in demand worldwide due to the decimated European and Japanese fleets.

The subsidies of the act were like a needle in the arm to shipping interests, and they became hooked. The Merchant Marine Act told shipowners, shipbuilders, and crews, "High cost really doesn't matter. We need you to build fast and big for the war effort." After the war, the inefficient, subsidized U.S. merchant marine remained profitable for a time because the world needed U.S. products at almost any cost.

Gradually, however, historic maritime powers rebuilt their fleets and reasserted themselves in the transport market. Milwaukee port director Ken Szallai says, "Suddenly U.S. shipping interests found themselves in a competitive dogfight that they were not in any way prepared to win. They were fat; they were bloated. They got a little boost from the Vietnam War, and that was that: the bloom was off the rose."

So what did they do? U.S shipping turned to the federal government for more subsidies, of course! The government responded by, among other things, using tax dollars to pay excessive freight rates on government cargo. Again, shippers found it was easier to lobby the government for money than to compete in the marketplace.

The Port That Wouldn't Die

Like most Great Lakes ports, the port of Milwaukee was slowly expiring in the 1970s and early 1980s. In 1986, Ken Szallai took over and redesigned the way the port did business. Port management began to be critical of itself, to ask if it was providing value to its customers, if it was doing things as efficiently as possible. It asked former customers why they left; it asked prospective customers what it could do for them. Port management even learned to ask what its services cost, something it had never done before! The port began doing what Big Steel has avoided doing for the last fifty years: competing.

In a few short years, Szallai helped Milwaukee build one of the most efficient grain-moving operations in the country. Then the federal government cut Milwaukee out of grain shipping. So it became the most efficient port at handling steel. Again federal laws pulled the rug out from under the operation. Still, the port of Milwaukee survives and even thrives because it has developed a diverse commodity portfolio that anticipates and manages for long-term trends. It handles its commodities and customers with an efficiency and attentiveness that keeps them coming back.

In the last ten years the port of Milwaukee has more than doubled its tonnage; 1995 was its biggest year since the mid-1960s. In eight of the last ten years the port has turned an operating profit. It generates $5 million in state and local taxes, despite the federal regulations and trade barriers that stunt commerce in U.S. port cities.

Cities, especially those with management expertise such as Milwaukee has enjoyed, would produce far more wealth for the United States if special-interest trade restrictions were relaxed or abolished.

Stirring the Melting Pot

The federal government perpetually misunderstands the complex relationship of cities to the economy. Cities are the soil in which commerce grows. One ingredient vital to such growth is people. Immigration has always been a source of strength for cities. Those who uproot themselves from their native countries to seek a better life in the United States tend to be highly motivated. They work hard and add new energy, customs, ideas, and products to the U.S.

City-States

economy. Overly restricting the movement of people is as detrimental to city life as is restricting the exchange of goods.

By way of illustration, let's look at New York City. Why did New York City become great and remain so? What was its recipe? Granted, its location features a protected ocean harbor and two major rivers. Yet dozens of other U.S. cities enjoy similar features, and many could argue that they are more ideally situated for prosperity than is New York.

New York became great because it let everyone in. It became great because of the incredible comingling of people, talents, and cultures that occurred at America's jumping-off point. For a variety of reasons, both intentional and accidental, other East Coast cities developed more homogeneity and, consequently, more limited economic potential. Other cities excluded certain religious or ethnic groups, or built themselves on specific industries, such as cotton, textiles, and the slave trade. The diverse people of New York pursued anything and everything. When one enterprise failed, two more sprang up to take its place. New York's ability to reinvent itself proved the source of its durability.

A 1996 report by the New York City Planning Department, titled "The Newest New Yorkers," suggests that the diversity that built New York City's economy in the nineteenth century remains a major ingredient in its success today. The city has seen a 32 percent increase in immigration in the 1990s, compared with the 1980s, contributing to a population increase of 3.5 percent since the beginning of the decade. According to the *New York Times*, "City officials presented the report's findings as confirmation of the contribution immigrants have made to the city's resurgence." Mayor Rudolph Giuliani hailed the report as proof that immigrants have been "the key to [New York's] success."

A recent publication of the U.S. Department of Housing and Urban Development seems to recognize what the Immigration and Naturalization Service and Congress often do not: the 1980s brought more immigrants to the United States than has any decade since 1900–10, and this immigration has played several key roles in boosting the U.S. economy. The simple fact that more people now live in the United States means an increase in the domestic market for goods and services as well as in the availability of labor. Also, these immigrants serve as foundations for international business relationships between the United States and their homelands. There is a crucial link between free trade and immigration; both encourage diversity that fuels the market.

Federal interference with immigration impedes the ability of big cities to generate wealth. Such restrictions promote homogeneity and stagnation. Federal interference in free trade hurts cities in the same way. It narrows options; it promotes stagnation and quashes the economic freedom that results in prosperity. Removing protectionist trade policies and excessive limitations on immigration would allow U.S. cities to add great value to the U.S. economy.

C H A P T E R   E I G H T

Clean City, Rich City

IMAGINE FOR A MOMENT what would happen if New York City were abolished and every New Yorker were evacuated to a new suburban home on a two-acre lot. The eight million displaced New Yorkers would gobble up sixteen million acres of previously undeveloped land. Half of that again would be needed for roads and streets, and even more for commercial and retail, plus, of course, parking.

Abolishing New York City would spread the economy out over thousands of square miles. Ex–New Yorkers would hop in their new cars whenever they wanted to go to work, the store, school, church, the park, the doctor, even just to see a neighbor a few houses away. Sewer lines, electric service, and roads would have to be extended to accommodate these new residents. To fit in with their neighbors, they'd grow luxurious, herbicide-laden grass on their large lots and mow it every week with pollution-spewing mowers. On weekends, they'd grill meat over charcoal ignited with toxic lighter fluid.

Cities are, on balance, good for the environment. New Yorkers pollute far less, on average, than their suburban neighbors. More gasoline is needed to support the automobile-dependent lifestyle; more electricity must be generated to heat and cool the large, stand-alone homes; more resources must be used to provide roads, pipes, and utility lines to the scattered sites; more energy must be consumed to supply water and return sewage from homes farther and farther away from municipal plants; more trucks must use more gas to move products farther and farther; more chemicals are applied to control the weeds on larger and larger lawns and more water to keep those lawns green; and, most important, more land must be cleared and leveled to accommodate the same amount of living.

Cities act much like wetlands in their ability to contain, filter, and process the by-products of human activity. A wetland is an incredibly complex, diverse biological system. It hosts an array of life and operates as a natural sponge to absorb and clean bad material from the environment. Not until recently, however, were wetlands appreciated. Thirty years ago they were considered nothing more than bogs, swamps, or wastelands, and people thought the best thing to be done with them was to reclaim them, meaning drain them, fill them in with truckloads of dirt, and transform them into productive uses. The federal government created a Bureau of Reclamation to expedite the process.

Our central cities were experiencing a similar situation thirty years ago. They were being drained of their natural wealth, destroyed by urban renewal, and wrenched into something they were not meant to be.

Today, environmental activists aren't the only people who appreciate wetlands. Children learn about wetlands in school; people donate money to wetlands protection groups; armchair nature lovers watching the Discovery Channel nod in agreement at shows extolling the virtues of wetlands. Yet too often these same well-intentioned nature lovers fail to understand the value of cities in absorbing human activity that would otherwise spread over and degrade the natural landscape.

"Green space" is the cry of many nature lovers. Green space is good. But an important key to preserving green space is to use it to preserve cities, not to spread them out. As former Madison, Wisconsin, mayor Paul Soglin remarked, "There are two types of environmentalists—those who understand the city is part of the environment, and those who don't."

Frederick Law Olmsted, a landscape architect who designed parks in New York City, Cleveland and Columbus, Ohio, Buffalo, New

Clean City, Rich City

York, Milwaukee, and dozens of other U.S. towns and cities, recognized the need for urban green space and helped create it without repudiating the integrity of the urban environment. Olmsted designed Manhattan's Central Park and Brooklyn's Prospect Park in New York City as natural topography adjacent to the most densely packed urban space in the United States. The stark contrast between the towers of Manhattan and Central Park is spectacular and attractive.

An approach to green space that doesn't work well demands larger and larger lots and more and more space between buildings, which creates houses in civic isolation surrounded by lawns. As author James Howard Kunstler notes, assembling "100 little country manors on 50 acres of land . . . doesn't add up to an authentic town."

Environmentalists need to take a deeper look at how cities function. Proximity is a magnifier, a catalyst that helps culture and commerce blossom when diverse people interact. But the proximity that catalyzes the magic of the marketplace in cities also precipitates inevitable unwelcome by-products. Crime, fire, congestion, and pollution—phenomena that occur everywhere—are magnified when people live and work close together. Yet precisely because of the concentration of these negative by-products of human life in cities, cities are able to deal with them effectively.

The massive, efficient sewer systems of cities, for example, result in far less pollution per person than do the septic systems scattered across the suburban and rural landscape, many of which leak contaminants into the groundwater. In cities, street and storm sewers absorb runoff and funnel it to treatment plants and sanitary sewers collect and treat human waste.

The diverse transportation systems of cities help city dwellers pollute less than those who embrace the automobile culture of our sprawling suburbs. The compact utility network delivers energy needs efficiently, avoiding unnecessary transmission costs. Well-laid street grids reduce travel distances. People living in urban apartment buildings, duplexes, or condos use less energy to heat and cool their living spaces. All these elements of a city—sewers, utility lines, street grids, transit systems, even apartment houses—should be viewed similarly to the diverse plants of a wetland; they contain and strain from the environment the potentially polluting by-products of life.

We now have the technology to build wetlands. Developers and governments can create wetlands to filter out toxins from rivers and drainage areas. Support for such projects is growing; people feel good about planting wetland grasses as natural cleansers. People should feel the same way whenever they see the city repairing a sewer line or adding a transit line—the equivalent of planting wetland grasses to keep the environment clean.

AN EFFECTIVE WAY for the federal government to protect the environment is to change policies that harm cities. We know that cities are good for the environment. It follows that the free market, which operates best in cities, is good for the environment as well. What a good application of federal effort it would be to allow cities to thrive by pursuing market-based environmental protection.

Much of the federal effort in this respect need not cost money or build bureaucracy. Less can be more: less spent on urban freeways to spread people out; less subsidization of exurban home building. By eliminating government-financed disincentives to proximity, federal policy makers can allow cities to thrive and help keep our natural environment clean.

It would be convenient for me, a believer in a free market, to assert that the environment would be best served through complete laissez-faire, but some government intervention is necessary to protect the natural resources that belong to all of us. As economist Milton Friedman says, "The preservation of the environment and the avoidance of undue pollution are real problems and the government has an important role to play." Friedman believes that the free-market system is essentially good for the environment, but that

Clean City, Rich City

many environmental costs have longer-term effects than the marketplace can measure. Carefully designed government participation allows free enterprise and environmental protection to go hand in hand, complementing one another. As free enterprise enhances living standards and fosters prosperity, particularly in urban areas, the environment shares in the benefits.

Economist Lester Thurow supports this view as well. In *The Zero Sum Society*, Thurow maintains that the free market best generates wealth and that a clean environment is a desirable commodity for wealthy countries and for upper-middle-class individuals. These individuals advocate for a clean environment because they have leisure and means to do so. People who are poor have other priorities—putting food on the table, keeping a roof over their heads, and acquiring the basic necessities of life and perhaps some fundamental creature comforts. "We have simply reached the point," Thurow claims, "where, for many Americans, the next item on their acquisitive agenda is a cleaner environment."

The free-market system generally promotes a clean environment through efficient use of the ingredients of production, but even within this positive framework the environment is bound to suffer from the actions of abusers. Government's most legitimate role is to prevent such abuse. Even conservative governments are starting to recognize the need for market intervention, as expressed by Nicholas Ridley, environment secretary under British Prime Minister Margaret Thatcher:

> *Pollution, like fraud, is something you impose on others against their will so that you can perhaps gain financial advantage. It is an ill for which the operation of the free market provides no automatic cure. Like the prevention of violence and fraud, pollution control is essentially an activity which the State . . . has to regulate and police.*

I agree with Ridley except in one respect: he misplaces the blame for pollution. Blaming free enterprise for pollution is like blaming the bank for bank robbers. Profiting by pollution is like clubbing people over the head and stealing their money. If government doesn't protect its citizens from such violations and uphold their rights, it is the government, not the free market, that has failed.

It is the proper role of government in a free society to protect the rights of its citizens, and these include the right to enjoy unpolluted air, land, and water. Environmental protection is one of the few areas in which the federal government needs to take the lead. The reason for this is simple:our rivers cross municipal and state lines; our groundwater aquifers know no boundaries; our air rides jet streams that render political boundaries irrelevant.

How can the government most effectively protect the environment with the least disruption to the free-market economy and, indirectly, to cities, natural allies of the environment? Traditionally, the federal government has assumed the role of setting and enforcing environmental standards. Laws and standards establish the parameters of acceptable behavior, yet standards set at achievable levels usually do not work as well as market-based incentives. Polluters who can easily meet environmental standards do so, and only marginal benefit occurs. Those who cannot meet the standards either cheat or go out of business, neither of which is a desirable option. Left in the market are (1) cheaters who won't improve their behavior, and (2) others who could probably improve further but have no incentive to do so.

Another problem with the standard-enforcement method of environmental protection is that its effective administration requires a huge bureaucracy, and the process-oriented nature of a bureaucracy tends to generate paperwork, rules and regulations, and complexity. This situation frustrates business executives, farmers, and everyday citizens seeking to run their operations or live their lives responsibly. It disrupts the marketplace, inhibits entrepreneurism, and costs tax dollars. It can also build a crutch under ways of doing business that are less efficient, blocking creation of new processes and businesses that might otherwise be invented by necessity.

Clean City, Rich City

Just as traditional government budgeting has measured inputs rather than outcomes, so bureaucracies have set up environmental standards that micromanage inputs rather than results. The Clinton administration has begun to address this problem with a new task force designed to streamline environmental regulations. The goal is to do a better job of setting result-based environmental standards and allowing individuals and businesses more flexibility in achieving those standards.

Although it is necessary to have standards and enforcement to protect the environment from abuse by polluters, it is even better to weave environmental protection into the very fabric of the free market so that it is an inevitable consequence of the economy at work.

The World Bank and the United Nations are looking at new ways to measure gross national product (GNP) that take the natural environment into account, literally. GNP traditionally measures the money, goods, and services moving through the economy. Theoretically, the higher the GNP, the better off a nation and its people. What GNP fails to measure is sustainability; that is, GNP fails to account for the depletion that results from production and consumption. Economists are working on ways to measure sustainable growth. Norway has adopted such a measurement, and other nations may soon follow.

A second market-based way in which the federal government can help protect the environment is to institute pollution pricing, in which the price of a product accurately reflects the cost of producing, using, and disposing of that product. Pollution pricing would drastically reduce the income, property, and payroll taxes that now subsidize the hidden production costs of polluters; it would allow consumers, through their purchasing power, to reward efficient producers; and it would encourage continuing market attention to environmental protection. Such market measures for pollution control would also recognize the value of cities in preserving the environment.

THE WEALTH OF CITIES

A third market-based way in which the government can help both cities and the environment is by removing obstacles to corporations' locating in central cities. People like to work in clean and attractive places, which is why so many corporate office parks are built on relatively pristine land on the urban fringe. Yet not only does this practice ruin previously undeveloped land, it also works directly against the environment-friendly density and efficiency of urban markets.

On both state and federal levels recent legislation is helping reverse this trend toward dispersal. This legislation bolsters market activity, helps cities, and aids the environment by cleaning up polluted, vacant, usually urban land and putting it back into productive use.

The term *brownfields* describes abandoned, contaminated industrial land, much of it in central-city locations. Until recently, such land usually remained abandoned. Neither private investors nor local governments devoted enough funds to clean up contaminated land or even to investigate land suspected of being contaminated. Although state and federal liability laws include strict cleanup standards, liability can easily be shifted from the landowner to others. Consequently, large tracts of urban land languish as brownfields. Rather than assume the risks of locating at former industrial sites, industries have built among the cornfields of the urban fringe, thus creating, over time, more brownfields over more land.

An emerging consensus holds that it is better environmental and economic policy to invest in the cleanup of urban sites than to continue to disperse industry and economic activity. Punitive liability laws are being moderated. Definitions of "contamination" are being revised. And standards for cleanup are being changed. It is important that brownfields be remediated to a standard that protects the health of future generations on and near the site, but a return to absolute purity is too much to expect.

Minnesota enacted the first brownfields program in 1988, and since that time more than half the nation's states have followed suit with varying degrees of effectiveness, easing legal liabilities and allowing site-specific cleanup techniques.

The state and federal governments must take primary responsibility for environmental protection, of course, but cities must be engaged as partners in the process. Cities that recognize and protect their environmental assets reap big rewards. Wichita, Kansas, for example, is waging and winning its own battle with contaminated sites, and its efforts are revitalizing the Old Town area. Efforts in Chattanooga, Tennessee, to clean up, protect, reforest, and develop the downtown have reversed a downward trend in real-estate values. Cities across the United States are engaging in a variety of strategies that link environmental protection and economic vigor. One common strategy is to rediscover their roots.

Today U.S. cities are putting renewed emphasis on the activities that created them. Financial, health, and educational services are growing; tourism is booming; and the nonprofit sector is also adding to the general financial health of cities. Clean air and water can provide an additional benefit that enhances cities' missions or processes.

Portland, Oregon, has implemented land-use controls and transit-oriented development to protect its natural environment and augment the vitality of the city. The four levels of government in Portland (region, county, suburb, city) work together to resist the negative antiurban trends of post–World War II society. The government understands that it cannot encourage transit use by trying to force people out of their cars; rather, it tries to influence the prevailing development equations. Portland's transit options and zoning philosophies encourage transit-oriented development without penalizing automobile users. As a result, much of Portland's development occurs in the central business district. Most of the people who travel to downtown Portland still use cars, but the valence has changed. Transit use is rising, not falling. Ridership on Portland's Metropolitan Area Express (MAX) light-rail system has grown by 50 percent in the last nine years. So many people use the transit system that a lively pedestrian environment has evolved. Portland's downtown bustles day and night. After business hours and on weekends pedestrians energize the streets, enjoying the pleasures of urban life. As a recent *Wall Street Journal* article summarized, "Portland has succeeded perhaps more than any other Western city in controlling urban sprawl, fostering public transportation and revitalizing the inner city." Because of the level of transit use and compact development, Portland's air is that much cleaner and its natural environment that much more intact, adding to its attractiveness.

Metropolitan Portland's zoning regulations include a development boundary, called the urban growth boundary (UGB). Drawn far enough out to accommodate natural growth, the boundary has gained popular acceptance. Although there is plenty of space to develop within the boundary, Portland-area development would be much more scattered without it. In his book, *Portland,* Carl Abbot explains, "Even though the Urban Growth Boundary looks permissive at first glance, it immediately forced changes in comprehensive planning in all three [Portland area] counties and became an important tool for limiting sprawl."

Portland's boundary came about only after a long political struggle in Oregon. In the late 1960s, Tom McCall succeeded Governor Mark Hatfield. Both were moderate Republicans who believed strongly in conservation.

During his term McCall became famous for warning Californians to stay away from his state because they were ruining Oregon's natural and social environments. He associated sprawl with the diseases of "Californism" and "Californication." While most governors were acting as shills for their tourism industries, Tom McCall disinvited Californians, the major component of Oregon's tourist population. The anti-California campaign didn't have the intended result, as it merely increased the desire of Californians to visit the forbidden state. It did, however, raise the consciousness of Oregon residents about conserving their state's natural beauty.

Governor McCall's commitment to the environment had a profound impact. He made it a priority to preserve the natural advan-

Clean City, Rich City

tages of his state and its cities through sound zoning and development policies. It was an arduous task. The notion that anyone should be able to build anything anywhere at any time runs just as deep in Oregon as it does in the rest of the United States. Nonetheless, McCall managed to make inroads against strong opposition from developers. In 1969, Oregon adopted a law requiring local governments to prepare land-use plans meeting ten specific guidelines. In 1973, McCall succeeded in strengthening the bill, creating the Land Conservation Development Commission to monitor local compliance with state land-use goals.

McCall's successor, Bob Straub, continued to advocate for land preservation. One of Straub's most memorable actions was to request that the federal government remove the proposed construction of the Mount Hood freeway from the interstate highway system plan. The people of Portland and their mayor, Neil Goldschmidt, supported Straub's action.

After serving as transportation secretary under President Jimmy Carter, Neil Goldschmidt was elected governor of Oregon in 1986. He further strengthened the concept of development boundaries. He also changed Oregon's transportation priorities, to the benefit of both cities and the environment.

Portland citizens have enjoyed intelligent, bipartisan political leadership with respect to environmental issues at the state and local levels. Portland's prosperity offers living proof that federal policies that degrade cities can be resisted and overcome.

Although Portland's efforts have centered on transit and land use, other cities are rediscovering the value of clean water. Most big cities are located near a reliable source of water, a river, lake, or ocean. Cities were established near water so that it could serve as their communication and commerce link with the world.

In the mid-nineteenth century, when railroads rendered water transportation less dominant, cities made the big mistake of literally turning their backs on the water that spawned them. Waterfront streets were abandoned. Buildings that once faced the river were converted to face away. Urban rivers were forgotten. Many waterways became little more than sewers, serving as dumping grounds for human and industrial waste. The Cuyahoga River in Cleveland, Ohio, became so polluted that it caught fire in 1969.

Today cities are rediscovering the value of their rivers and lakes. The Riverwalk in San Antonio, Texas, is a prime tourist attraction. The Cuyahoga River is now the entertainment center of northern Ohio. Baltimore has attracted millions of dollars of commercial and residential investment near its inner harbor. Cities such as Boston, whose waterfront Faneuil Hall marketplace is flanked by housing, learned the lesson earlier and have enjoyed thriving waterfronts for some time.

In Milwaukee, too, we're bringing people back to the water. We believe that one of the best ways for a city to protect its natural resources is to drive market demand. When people walk, talk, work, eat, drink, boat, and play by the water, when it becomes part of their day-to-day life and not merely a special-occasion destination, a real constituency for clean water is created.

At the turn of the century, architects Daniel Burnham and Alfred Clas recommended that Chicago and Milwaukee build river walks. Chicago built Wacker Drive. But Milwaukee's plans languished until the late 1980s.

When fully constructed in 1998, the river walk will feature a two-mile, continuous walkway along the Milwaukee River. The plan is not very different from what Burnham and Clas envisioned nearly a hundred years ago.

The benefits of the river walk are already evident in downtown Milwaukee. Not long ago, if you saw boaters on the Milwaukee River you assumed they were just passing through on the way to beautiful Lake Michigan. The river was a forbidding place, with banks lined with the bleak, gray backs of buildings, dumpsters, trash, and crumbling parking lots.

Today boaters cruise up and down the river as if on promenade. People wave to the mariners from riverside restaurants and pubs. Scullers race between city bridges strung with lights. Where once ac-

Clean City, Rich City

cess was restricted, families take evening strolls. Long-empty buildings have been converted to condominiums that have occupancy waiting lists. Commercial establishments are renting out loft apartments on their upper floors. The new river dwellers consider the river their front yard. Their buildings are painted bright colors, and fire escapes now double as porches, holding flower pots and grills.

Three miles north of downtown, the city permanently opened the gates of a dam that had been closed for 150 years. During those years debris, sediment, and chemicals settled to the bottom of the eighty-acre impoundment behind the dam. The stagnant water over the toxic mud baked in the sun, nurtured algae and bacteria, and turned into a soupy mess filled with only the lowest forms of aquatic life, such as bullheads, suckers, clams, and carp.

Within a few months of opening the dam gates, a clean, swift channel replaced the impoundment. Game fish, such as lake trout, steelheads, and salmon, migrated in from Lake Michigan. The newly exposed mudflats erupted into wetland vegetation reaching five and six feet high.

Now fishing enthusiasts line the banks of the river and the meanderings of city residents have created footpaths. Opening the dam gates added value to the city by helping clean the environment. More important, it helped solidify a constituency for clean water, as people have begun to care about the river again.

Seven years ago, I'd get only a handful of complaints per year about Milwaukee River pollution. Virtually no one cared. Now, even though its water quality has measurably improved, I get dozens of complaints each month about the river. People now consider it an asset worth improving.

PEOPLE ENJOY ABUNDANT, some say inexhaustible, air and water resources, but the amount of land on Earth is more limited. Many state and federal policies degrade cities and disperse people and businesses across the limited available land. These policies encourage inefficient consumption of our natural resources and work against sustainable economic growth. They also impede the ability of future generations to decide how to use the earth and its resources.

U.S. cities, ravaged by heavy-handed federal transportation policies and special-interest exploitation of the environment, search for economic and environmental answers. Portland, Oregon, is leading the way with antisprawl zoning and a protransit strategy. Even Los Angeles, the birthplace of sprawl, has built three transit lines and is encouraging compact development with its new downtown plan.

Increasingly, environmentalists are uniting with urban advocates and developers to forge a common vision of (1) urban life as a big part of the answer to environmental challenges and (2) environmentalism as a big part of the answer to the challenges of cities.

The Congress for New Urbanism is an organization of architects, and developers dedicated to restore the urban form to popularity and to oppose the spread of strip sprawl to more U.S. land.

The International Council for Local Environmental Initiatives (ICLEI), an international group of cities associated with the United Nations, also ties urbanism and environmentalism together. ICLEI views halting the spread of suburban sprawl as the key to addressing the potential calamity of global warming.

The Equitable Life Insurance Company has begun to rate real-estate investment prospects in metro areas using both environmental and quality-of-urban-life criteria. These measures guide the real-estate decisions of their investment portfolio. The smear of pop-up development on the edges of U.S. metropolitan areas is less attractive as an investment than it once was—new evidence that clean cities will be the rich cities of the twenty-first century.

C H A P T E R   N I N E

U.S. Autobahns

PEOPLE, PLACES, AND PRODUCTS are the ingredients that, when mixed together in a city, generate wealth and, in turn, culture and religion.

Nothing could be better calculated to destroy this recipe than the current U.S. transportation policy. In 1957, Congress passed, and President Eisenhower signed, appropriations for the Interstate Highway Act. Hailed as the dawn of a glowing new age in transportation, the act was to augment state highways with a network of limited-access highways. A federal gasoline tax paid for 90 percent of the system's construction and maintenance costs, states paid 10 percent, and cities nothing.

Planner Lewis Mumford was among but a handful who greeted this dawn with umbrella in hand. He predicted that the policy of freeway building would do more damage to U.S. cities than all the bombing of World War II had done to European cities: "When the American people, through their Congress, voted . . . for a twenty-six-billion-dollar highway program," he said, "the most charitable thing to assume about this action is that they hadn't the faintest notion what they were doing. Within the next fifteen years they will doubtless find out; but by that time it will be too late to correct all the damage to our cities."

Since 1957 the federal government has spent trillions of dollars on multilane freeways that slice through complex networks of urban avenues, boulevards, streets, and alleys like chainsaws. People, products, and places sit stranded and strangled by freeways—the very ties intended to bind. Freeways have subtracted homes and businesses from the city and dispersed millions of U.S. citizens and businesses to the suburbs. Classic urban transportation systems, including rail, streetcars, and trolleybuses, once privately financed and operated, have been undermined by the federally subsidized intrusion of freeways.

These new roads have left in their wake vast wastelands in New York City's South Bronx, Cleveland, Ohio's west side, Cincinnati, Ohio's West End, and countless other cities, some of which are just now struggling to regain some degree of vitality. Then there's Detroit, where every freeway ever planned was built.

My parents honeymooned in Detroit in 1946, guests of a grateful government that provided a week in a hotel to those who were POWs during World War II. My parents could choose between Minneapolis or Detroit. Since they lived in St. Paul, Minnesota, they chose Detroit.

They stayed at the luxurious Book Cadillac Hotel. With a new Bell and Howell movie camera my father recorded the first days of an enduring marriage and the heyday of downtown Detroit. At that time, Detroit bustled with pedestrians and shoppers in scenes reminiscent of the great cities of Europe. Three department stores—Hudsons, Kerns, and Crowleys—all on Cadillac Square, rivaled Manhattan's Bloomingdale's, Macy's, and Gimbels. Detroit's prominent skyline was surpassed only by those of Chicago and New York.

Fifty years later, Detroit has changed beyond recognition. The pedestrians are gone. The streetcars, with the exception of a small, antique replica that operates occasionally, are gone. The department stores are gone. Most buildings are gone or boarded up. The twenty-eight-story Book Cadillac, now padlocked, has joined the Detroit acropolis of empty skyscrapers.

If money is the measure, the federal government kept faith with Detroit during its decline. But if results matter, Washington's dollars were fool's gold. Billions flowed from Washington into Detroit in the form of concrete—the freeways that Lewis Mumford feared. Billions more built public housing in the city and tax-subsidized middle-class housing in the suburbs. More was spent on urban renewal and parking lots—so many parking lots that there are not many places left to visit.

Hope springs eternal. New leadership from a dedicated new mayor, Dennis Archer, gives reason to believe that Detroit could thrive again. Baseball and football stadiums are in the works. In 1994, thirty-nine single-family housing permits were issued, ending a thirty-year drought. In 1995, sixty-seven such permits were issued. Yet construction is still dwarfed by destruction. Detroit demolished 5,994 dwellings in 1995, a number that recalls the bombing of Rotterdam in 1940.

GEORGE KENNAN, foreign-policy scholar and former ambassador to the Soviet Union and Yugoslavia, was born and raised in Milwaukee. In 1990 he returned to receive an honorary degree from the University of Wisconsin-Milwaukee.

Kennan arrived a day early to tour his hometown, which he had not seen for forty years. As mayor, I accompanied him. We visited various landmarks and fondly remembered sites from Kennan's youth. Although some were gone, he delighted in those remaining. We ended our tour at one of Kennan's favorite boyhood spots, a small, downtown park.

In Kennan's youth, train stations had abutted the park on three sides: the Milwaukee Electric Railway; Milwaukee Union Station, proud home of the Hiawatha; and the North Shore Railway, the one-hundred-mile-per-hour electric train that connected Milwaukee to Chicago in only seventy minutes. In those days, when young Kennan finished his paper route, if he had extra papers, he would bike to the park. To him, the park seemed like the center of the world, with thousands of passengers coming and going. It was a basic city park, surrounded by buildings full of human activity, making its little green common all the more valuable. Kennan would sell his papers, all of them, fast, and he had great fun doing so among the excitement and crowds generated by the nearby trains, hotels, restaurants, offices, shoeshine stands, and saloons.

That day in 1990, Kennan stood in what is now called Zeidler Park and his eyes moistened. All three train stations were gone. The park was empty and quiet. The only sound was the roar of the freeway a block away. Kennan looked off toward a concrete parking ramp. He shook his head and said, "This is not an improvement."

The degradation of U.S. cities was no accident. Nor was it inevitable. It was planned. Some of our most talented architects and planners knew exactly what was happening.

When he conceived the limited-access divided-highway system that he named the interstate, engineer Norman Bel Geddes asserted that it should not trespass cities. He warned us in his 1940 book, *Magic Motorways:*

> *[I]f the purpose of the motorway as now conceived is that of being a high-speed, non-stop thoroughfare, the motorway would only bungle the job if it got tangled up with the city. . . . A great motorway has no business cutting a wide swath right through a town or city and destroying the values there; its place is in the country.*

Americans who travel through Canada, Europe, or the Pacific Rim often comment on how interesting and exciting the cities there are; senior travelers say they are reminded of what U.S. cities once looked like. A visit to London, Paris, or Tokyo proves that urban centers can and do thrive in the modern world. A visit to Toronto, just 250 miles east of Detroit, shows that U.S. cities didn't have to turn out as they have.

To understand how other developed nations emerged from the postwar era with cities that function well and look even better, we need to understand how limited-access divided highways disperse

U.S. Autobahns

people and devalue cities while creating congestion and what series of events combined to encourage freeway construction and the destruction of transit. With this knowledge we can investigate how traditional city street and grid systems absorb and reduce traffic congestion and suggest federal policies to temper the destructive effects of urban freeways.

The tendency of freeways to disperse people works directly against the natural advantage of a city. By spreading people and activity over greater and greater distances, freeways undermine the critical mass that makes urban economies so productive. Although some urban sprawl is inevitable, freeways have accelerated and extended suburbanization.

In *The Fractured Metropolis,* Jonathan Barnett puts suburbanization in a historical context. He notes that the original suburbs of the great European cities were poor, as they comprised people and commercial practices that were undesirable and hence forced outside the walled cities. Eventually, walled protection was not a necessity. As early as the sixteenth century, people of means in London began setting up residential districts just beyond the crowds and dirt of the urban core. These affluent districts shifted the geographic focus of the marketplace. Providers of goods and services established themselves near the money. What had been a residential neighborhood of the aristocracy was soon transformed into a market district. Then the well-to-do residents climbed into their carriages and moved a half step farther out.

Suburbanization was originally so difficult to distinguish from urbanization that the first official use of the term *suburb* didn't appear until the 1880 census. At that time, U.S. suburbs typically consisted of tightly packed homes along trolley lines or on local streets. Most suburbanites could easily walk downtown.

The primary difference between the suburbanization that took place before World War II and the suburbanization that has run rampant since is speed. Hundreds of years of moderate, natural expansion within the orbit of urban commerce picked up steam in

1920 and exploded into outright sprawl with the advent of the freeway system.

New York City, the most densely populated metropolis in the United States, is the product of prefreeway suburbanization turned urbanization. The city crawled north from behind Wall Street, establishing mixed residential and market districts as it expanded, each step no more than a carriage ride beyond the previous one. Even the older suburbs of New York, Chicago, and most eastern and midwestern cities are urban in density and form.

Although roads and automobiles are convenient scapegoats for the unraveling of the urban fabric, automobiles are by no means evil. We need them. They are an important element in every nation's transportation system. But they should be only one element of many. As Mumford wrote, "The fatal mistake we have been making is to sacrifice every other form of transportation to the private motorcar." We have overaccommodated the auto at the expense of other methods of transportation.

Modern road building had its start with a Scotsman named McAdam. In the early 1800s McAdam devised a way of surfacing roads with gravel and tar to make them better suited to the heavier and faster coaches of the day. A road laid down by this process is known as macadam, after its inventor.

As landscape architect Sylvia Crowe explains, however, McAdam's influence extended well beyond the contribution of a word to the language:

It was Macadam who made the revolutionary proposal that roads should be constructed to suit vehicles, instead of vehicles being designed for roads. Perhaps the trend is now due for the reverse, and vehicles should make some concessions to the physical limitations of land space.

With McAdam as their guide, early clubs of highway enthusiasts gradually became serious about dominating public policy. The earliest disciples were products of schools of planning and engineering. These institutions now spawn experts who promote the ideals of highway design and the idea of endless highway construction. Author Kenneth Schneider notes that professional traffic engineering has delayed "the stark realization that the automobile . . . is completely incompatible with the good city. Without traffic engineers, the automobile would have demonstrated its utter futility between 1920 and 1940, rather than in the 1970s."

Sprawl is the direct result of auto accommodation. In a vicious cycle of positive feedback, as author and sociologist Jane Jacobs calls it, auto accommodation generates effects that increase the need for further accommodation.

Engineers design freeways to enhance the movement of motor vehicles. Motor vehicles operate swiftly on straight, wide, flat surfaces. Everything that is not sufficiently straight, wide, and flat is, from a freeway-engineering perspective, in the way. This puts urban neighborhoods in the way, as they are not usually flat and wide, but compact, complicated, and dense. Charles Glover, research director of the Travel Research Association, a highway advocacy group, wrote in the late 1950s that "urban disorder must not be allowed to impair the function of the well designed highway."

So, avoiding disorder, a freeway slices straight through the city grid. The people and businesses it displaces must move, often to the urban periphery, where transportation options are limited. Cleveland's inner-belt freeway, for example, displaced nineteen thousand residents, many of whom moved to the suburban fringe. Freeway users eventually need to leave the freeway to get to their destinations. An exit ramp takes them onto a local street, which is widened to bear the increased load. These freeway commuters also must park somewhere, typically in large parking lots or garages, of which there are never enough. Valuable urban land is thus consumed in moving and storing automobiles. As more space is required to contain the same amount of activity, commerce spreads out, making travel by automobile even more necessary. Jacobs describes the

THE WEALTH OF CITIES

end result as "a great, thin smear, incapable of generating the metropolitan facilities, diversity and choices theoretically possible for the population and economy concerned."

What highway advocates call disorder often delights residents and tourists. Chinatown in San Francisco, the town squares in Savannah, Georgia, the French Quarter in New Orleans, and Greenwich Village in New York City confound through traffic while attracting billions of tourist dollars.

Less well known neighborhoods may not draw as many tourists, but they earn the love of their residents. Thirty years ago on Milwaukee's near north side, the corner of Eighth and Walnut defined the center of Bronzeville. This lively hub of African American culture was Milwaukee's modest version of Harlem's 125th and Lennox. The Regal theater, law offices, a pool hall, and nightclubs created a blend of commerce and culture. Prominent artists, such as Duke Ellington, would perform downtown and then hang out at the Flame in Bronzeville after hours.

In 1966 the state Department of Transportation decided to run what is now Interstate 43 through Bronzeville. Few people thought twice about this decision. Certainly no one with power did. Lawyer and state representative Lloyd Barbee picketed the first bulldozer in protest of what he called the "dirty ditch," but his action proved futile. Today Bronzeville has disappeared without a trace, except for an annual remembrance held in a nearby park.

Milwaukee's Italian community, concentrated in the Third Ward just southeast of downtown, wielded more clout than did Bronzeville. The Italians operated Milwaukee's still-vibrant wholesale food district.

So when the Wisconsin Department of Transportation (WisDOT) decided to construct I-794 through the Third Ward, the Italian residents resisted, at least for a while. Ultimately the supporters of "progress" prevailed, but not until WisDOT and the county agreed to place a monument to the demolished Church of Our Lady of Pompeii, which had been the spiritual center and chief landmark of

U . S . A u t o b a h n s

the Italian community. Two years after the elevated freeway was built, the neighborhood had declined so much that the city contemplated turning the remains of the Third Ward into a pornographic combat zone for strip joints and erotic book stores. This indignity was too much even for those who had supported progress, and the plan failed. Today the Third Ward prospers except in areas next to the noise and smell of the freeway, where most buildings have crumbled or been razed in favor of surface parking lots.

What helps cities thrive is what Jacobs calls "unplanned combinations of existing ideas." The spontaneous mingling of ideas and cultures spawns innovation and builds the economy. Freeways work against this valuable process. They are imposing physical obstacles that divide neighborhood from neighborhood so that, instead of enhancing cities, freeways devalue them. Downtowns end up confined, even isolated, by freeways intended to protect them from residential areas.

In addition, the urban roadways of the United States seem designed to be ugly as a matter of national policy. Interstate standards mandate the monotonous repetition: straight, wide, and flat, relieved only by reinforced-concrete cloverleafs built on pillars that raise autos above the life of the city. The smell and unrelenting noise of the freeway is so noxious to nearby residents that most U.S. cities now have large walls called sound barriers lining the roadway. If former East German Communists Walter Ulbricht and Erich Honecker came back to life in Berlin today they would be totally disoriented—the Berlin Wall is gone. But if they visited any large U.S. city they would feel right at home with its Sound Wall.

U.S. cities didn't have to choose these ugly freeways. Consider the beautiful Champs-Elysées in Paris, or handsome Connecticut Avenue in Washington, D.C. Both roads move large amounts of traffic, accommodate pedestrians, and allow the grid of cross streets to connect with the life of the city.

No one recognizes the ugliness of U.S. freeways more than the automobile manufacturers. Take a look at their commercials. Cars glide alone down tree-shaded country lanes or park on quaint city streets. They are never shown where they're most likely to be: stuck on a freeway.

By spreading the population out and forcing people to rely on their cars for every local travel need freeways exacerbate air pollution and thus further devalue cities. The Clean Air Act Amendments of 1990 require many large urban areas to meet standards or risk sanction. In southeastern Wisconsin, 60 percent of the ozone problem targeted by the Clean Air Act results from motor vehicles. The average city dweller—who lives closer to work, stores, schools, recreation, and most necessities of life—travels by automobile far less than the average suburbanite, yet it is urban residents and industries that suffer the consequences of the automobile-dependent lifestyle. If large cities can't reduce motor-vehicle emissions to acceptable human-health levels, they risk losing jobs as the antipollution obligation falls on industry.

Some people, including many traffic engineers, argue that more freeway lanes are the best remedy for pollution. They suggest that freeways reduce congestion by moving vehicles faster and therefore result in diminished air emissions. What they fail to take into account is that freeways induce more and longer trips. Instead of shopping locally, people hit the freeway to shop. It seems more convenient, until almost everyone does the same thing and then congestion and pollution become worse than ever.

A strong urban transit system is a better alternative. Many communities—including San Diego, Sacramento, and San Jose, California; Portland, Oregon; Buffalo; Baltimore; St. Louis; and, most recently, Dallas—have added light-rail transit to bus transit. Studies in Milwaukee have shown that a regional light-rail system could reduce harmful air emissions by 2 percent. Transit opponents scoff at a 2 percent improvement in air quality, yet many of them would scramble to achieve a 2 percent improvement in their cholesterol level or personal investment portfolio.

The 2 percent figure is merely a projection based on how many people would, by a certain date, use rail transit instead of a car for

U.S. Autobahns

certain trips. It does not consider the prospective long-term effects of rail transit on housing development and the location decisions of metropolitan-area businesses. Transit concentrates development. Look around North America. Cities with strong transit systems—Toronto, New York, Boston, Chicago, Portland, Oregon, and Vancouver, British Columbia—all boast healthy urban economies with concentrated development. Cities that have depended exclusively on highways to meet their transportation needs, such as Detroit and Houston, have sprawled all over the map.

A rail-transit system affects the prospective behavior of individuals more than it changes current behaviors. A certain number of people will change transportation modes immediately when transit becomes available. More important, people who have not yet developed transportation habits will have the opportunity to build transit into their lives. They will be able to choose to live near a transit line, not to spend money on that second car, or to reside in one of the compact neighborhoods that transit tends to generate. In most U.S. cities these choices are not available now.

Rediscovering avenues, boulevards, and streets is another alternative to freeway building. Arterial streets that meet a variety of public and private needs benefit cities. Property values along and near these streets tend to increase. Broadway in New York City, the Champs-Elysées in Paris, Wilshire Boulevard in Los Angeles, and Michigan Avenue in Chicago are examples of arterial streets that are thriving as a result of investment and impressive increases in property value.

Such benefits will accrue, however, only as long as a street retains its fundamental character. When a street is widened and access limited to help speed through traffic, use of the adjoining property changes. Residences, corner grocery stores, and businesses that rely on spontaneous customers or pedestrian traffic may locate elsewhere. As the arterial becomes one-dimensional, it loses its charm and, like a freeway, becomes a funnel for automobiles. Its value declines as traffic moves farther and farther between increasingly insignificant destinations.

THE WEALTH OF CITIES

San Francisco's experience with the Embarcadero Freeway serves as an example of urban value lost to automobile accommodation. Planners in post–World War II San Francisco called for the construction of an elevated expressway along the Embarcadero, the waterfront between the Bay Bridge and Fisherman's Wharf. Caspar Weinberger, then the state assemblyman for the neighborhood, fought the elevated freeway, claiming that it would destroy access to businesses and block the view of the bay, thereby reducing property values.

Weinberger lost the fight, but he was vindicated years later when the freeway was removed after incurring damage from the 1991 earthquake. In its place, an at-grade boulevard was built. Views of the bay, blocked for forty years, were restored. Property values along the Embarcadero have risen over 300 percent. Weinberger, well known as President Ronald Reagan's budget director and defense secretary, takes great delight in the fact that most of the people celebrating the Embarcadero's removal are liberal environmentalists who would be shocked to know that he fought construction of the road in the first place.

Weinberger does not believe that the Embarcadero is an isolated case. He suggests that "tearing down freeways and replacing them with boulevards may become one of the great public works endeavors of the twenty-first century." Additional examples abound. Boston's Central Artery project is burying a freeway and allowing downtown and the North End to reconnect. In Oregon, Portland's view of the Willamette River, once blocked by a freeway, has been restored by replacing the freeway with a boulevard; Manhattan's elevated West End Highway is also being replaced with a boulevard.

FREEWAYS DRAIN FROM cities more than people and businesses. They drain precious tax dollars from those who remain.

U.S. Autobahns

When automobiles arrived early in the century, Milwaukee mayor Dan Hoan noted, "It is said by our Comptroller that the automobile alone has cost our municipal government four million dollars a year for additional police officers, signals, playgrounds, street construction, et cetera, which is a new burden of expense. Of this cost, the automobile contributes, in reality, less than three hundred thousand dollars a year and the remainder adds to other taxation."

Today about 50 percent of Milwaukee's municipal levy is devoted to direct costs associated with motor vehicles, including construction and maintenance of roads and highways, interest on debt from earlier construction, and signage as well as police, street lighting, and sewer needs. This amounts to a direct property-tax subsidy of $106.7 million per year. This figure does not include indirect costs, such as neighborhood disruption, air and water pollution, and costs associated with accidents. Nor does it include taxes lost by removing land from the tax base to serve the automobile. Half the surface area of the average city—and two-thirds that of Los Angeles—is dedicated to automobile use.

Obviously a significant amount of road infrastructure must be in place to allow an urban economy to thrive. But exclusive auto use—encouraged by the direct ingress and egress of the freeway and throughway system—has made our urban transportation network far more expensive and far less efficient than necessary.

MOST URBAN superhighways were built in the late 1960s and early 1970s, which is about the time the term *freeway* came into vogue. The term means, I suppose, free of congestion, free of traffic lights, free of any barrier to free travel by the car. The name *freeway* also implies free in terms of cost—free of cost because the federal government paid 90 percent and the state government paid 10 percent for freeway construction. Because freeways cost nothing locally to build, their design and construction were virtually free and therefore exempt from the scrutiny of local taxpayers.

These freeways, however, could be expensive and elaborate. Milwaukee's Marquette interchange cost $81.7 million to build in 1966; in today's dollars that's $378.6 million. To rebuild just this one interchange to meet today's standards would cost up to $730 million—only thirty years after its construction! Much of the U.S. interstate system is reaching the end of its design life. As the federal government struggles with its financial deficit, it is becoming clear that freeways aren't free at all.

The Legacy of LBJ and Robert Moses

The election of Lyndon Baines Johnson to the United States Senate in 1948 was in many ways a turning point for U.S. cities. Johnson was so talented, so powerful, and so single-minded that almost everything he did, he did to excess, whether it was his war on North Vietnam, his war on poverty, his advocacy of civil rights, his pursuit of the interests of big oil, or his political alliance with the road-building industry.

Early in his career Johnson discovered that road builders like to contribute to political campaigns. The Texas road-building firm Brown and Root helped with Johnson's first congressional campaign.

In Texas at that time, road building seemed to be an unmixed blessing. Having grown up in the Pedernales River valley west of Austin, Johnson understood the need for all-weather farm-to-market roads. He had spent a summer working on a road gang, experiencing firsthand the hard labor and slim profit margins of the industry, as well as the satisfaction of helping farmers in a material way. It was only natural that an older, more powerful Johnson would help road building grow and expand.

Senator Albert Gore Sr., father of Vice President Albert Gore, was the chief sponsor of the Interstate Highway Act. But it was Johnson who, as senate majority leader, jammed funding for the act through Congress and later, as president, oversaw its rapid implementation. If Johnson hadn't been so good at legislating and so obsessive about every task he undertook; if the genteel U.S. Senate had reined him in; if Americans had elected a more assertive president than Eisenhower; if Johnson's ally Sam Rayburn hadn't run the House—if any of these conditions had been met, the federal share of highway-construction costs might not have reached 90 percent.

Before Johnson went to work, federal aid to state governments for road building was 50 percent, up from its original 20 percent, and states were still not biting. At those prices, paying for even half a superhighway was still too much for many states that were dealing with a mix of competing demands.

At the state and local levels, another power had emerged, New York City's Robert Moses. Although his direct sphere of influence extended only to state and local government, Moses had a profound and determinative effect on national and even international policy. Moses, who never drove a car, popularized the limited-access highway in the United States.

Robert Moses began building power in the 1920s. Originally appointed New York City parks commissioner, by 1950 he had become commissioner of just about everything that had to do with construction in both New York City and New York State. His legacy is well documented in Robert Caro's *The Power Broker*.

Moses didn't like the congestion of cities; he held the common, early-twentieth-century attitude that it was somehow bad for people to live close together. Moses saw blight in neighborhoods where people lived happily.

Moses did like roads and monumental buildings. He believed that roads were the main expression of public works and that public works were the means to some sort of utopian ideal. Tragically for cities, Moses had both the determination and the power to impose his will. In the process of fulfilling his vision, he had square miles of neighborhoods torn down. At times, such as during the construction of a highway in the East Tremont section of the Bronx, he seemed to go out of his way to have as many homes as possible removed. Moses believed that "to achieve integrity of automobile movement one must destroy living environments."

The urbanscapes Moses created—superblocks of public, high-rise apartment buildings surrounded by artificial greens—are virtually uninhabitable today. His was a type of architecture attractive to Communist countries in the 1950s through the 1970s: multiple-story, concrete apartment buildings lined up one after the other to assert through form and mass that the individual is but a cog in the machine of a utopian society.

Through will and talent Moses profoundly influenced a generation of transportation professionals both in the United States and abroad. As a consultant in the 1940s, Moses helped design the highway system for São Paulo, Brazil, then a city of a few hundred thousand. Today São Paulo has the worst traffic jams in South America, perhaps in the world.

Lyndon Johnson and Robert Moses, each in his own way, was driven by idealism toward a utopia that ultimately undermined the urban form. Not every influence on U.S. transportation was so idealistic.

General Motors (GM), acting in concert with its subsidiaries and allies in the oil and tire industries, intentionally destroyed private streetcar companies in most of the larger cities in the United States. In 1948, GM lost an antitrust case in federal court and was found guilty of illegally conspiring to render transit noncompetitive with the private automobile. GM was buying up rail-transit companies, ripping out the tracks, burning the railcars, and replacing them with gasoline and diesel buses. GM lost the antitrust case, but the court essentially allowed GM to win by limiting damages to ten thousand dollars.

GM's actions accelerated the decline in transit ridership, and private transit companies went bankrupt. In city after city ruined transit systems fell into the hands of local governments. Local gov-

U.S. Autobahns

ernments then had to subsidize bus systems that lost riders while the federal government continued to invest more dollars in freeways.

BY THE TIME the Interstate Highway Act became law, rural areas had been clamoring for improved auto access for two decades and large cities had been struggling to solve severe congestion challenges. But for the cities' disease, freeways turned out to be the wrong treatment, and consequently nearly killed the patients.

For a decade or so, from the time the Interstate Highway Act was authorized in 1944 until it was funded in 1957, a postwar idealism infused the transportation community. With the Great Depression and World War II over, planners and engineers collectively convinced themselves that higher ends were in order than mere pavement laying. A popular GM exhibit at the 1939 World's Fair in New York, designed by Norman Bel Geddes, laid out a model utopian city in which roadway-grade separations eliminated the need for traffic lights. This model captured the imagination of engineers and motorists worldwide.

Expanding on this idealism, the concept of the complete highway emerged in planning circles in 1943. It was the equivalent of the post–Civil War City Beautiful movement. For a brief time, beauty was considered one of four goals in the construction of any highway. Then the money started coming. The idealism of Bel Geddes was replaced by a feeding frenzy at the federal trough. "Just do it" and "Get it done" were the cries as Robert Moses and his counterparts across the United States lined up at the interstate spending spigot.

Whether it was because cities and urban neighborhoods put up the only resistance to just doing it, or whether it was for other, more deep-seated reasons, the highway crowd showed particular contempt for cities and their residents. These planners knew exactly what they were going to do to cities.

In 1959 highway-advocate Charles Glover warned cities what was coming.

The routes out of the city will be faster, safer and more attractive, but they will not control suburban sprawl or provide schools, water and other public utilities. . . . In other words, unless communities act quickly, the new highways may create serious problems for them.

The warning was not heard. Many cities, anxious to receive their fair share of federal money, eagerly participated in their own demise.

Joseph Ingraham's essay of this period, "Politics and Road Building," was not sympathetic. When he wasn't covering transportation issues for the *New York Times,* Ingraham was likely to be on Robert Moses' payroll. He revealed his contempt for cities when he called citizens' efforts to stop construction of the Cross-Bronx Expressway "some of the seamiest examples of political tampering."

Ingraham characterized opponents to urban freeways as small. In describing local businesses that were trying to save themselves, Ingraham wrote, "Highway planning is continually hampered by the perennial scrap between an established enterprise and the unbiased highway expert." His summary of the fight in the Bronx dismissed freeway opponents: "It is a typical big-city situation, and counterparts can be found in Chicago, Detroit, or any urban center where more roads are a paramount need."

One of those counterparts was found in Milwaukee in the person of Mayor Henry Maier, who accurately declared, "Construction is not proceeding . . . because the highway engineers planned these freeways from a purely highway engineering standpoint without any consideration whatsoever of what other impacts they would have on our community."

In *The Man with the Red and Green Eyes,* former Baltimore and New York City traffic commissioner Henry A. Barnes echoed Ingraham's contempt for people in cities. In the cover copy he complained,

U . S .   A u t o b a h n s

"Headaches are an occupational disease for the traffic commissioner . . . but when the amateurs start getting into the act then the pain is apt to spread to other portions of our anatomy."

Well, Ingraham and Barnes can rest easy now—they won. Detroit and the South Bronx have their roads and not much else.

The simmering undercurrent of anti-urban sentiment was finally publicly articulated in the late 1960s and early 1970s. After the riots in Detroit, the Watts section of Los Angeles, and elsewhere, the federal government endorsed a policy of dispersion.

In his 1972 State of the Union message Richard Nixon revealed his lack of appreciation for cities by saying, "We must create a new rural environment which will not only stem the migration to urban areas, but reverse it." What he did not say was that the migration had already been reversed by suburban subsidies, highway building, and contempt for poor and minority urban residents.

The National Governors' Conference supported Nixon's policy of population dispersal. In 1968 members passed a resolution identifying the source of the nation's ills: "Population imbalance is at the core of nearly every major social problem facing our nation today." The group urged "a more even distribution of population" among states. (One wonders if Utah residents really wanted people from the South Bronx to move to Ogden.)

Even the National League of Cities came out against cities. In 1969 the league called for a "specific policy for the settlement of people throughout the nation to balance the concentration of population among and within metro and non-metro areas."

James Sundquist's *Dispersing Population*, funded by the Brookings Institute, spells out, step-by-step, how to remove people from cities and spread them across the face of the map. In closing he states:

If the people of a democratic country want a pattern of population distribution less concentrated than that which results from the natural play of economic forces, there is no reason that they cannot have it. Through governmental action, the influences at work within the economy that make for concentration can be neutralized and those that make for deconcentration can be reinforced.

By the time the book was published in 1975, Sundquist's prescription had become a description.

IF WE LOOK BACK over the last fifty years it appears that U.S. cities, on balance, would have been better off if the federal government had stayed out of the surface-transportation business altogether. State and local governments would have made their own decisions, with their own money, whether to build highways and transit systems and how big to build them.

This is exactly what happened in Canada. There, the federal government generally kept out of provincial and local transportation decisions. Today all large Canadian cities have balanced transportation systems and healthy city centers. With no 90 percent federal gifts for divided, limited-access highways, Canadian cities chose to spend their money on a balance of roads and transit lines, which has both preserved and augmented the value of those cities. Toronto offers streetcars, trolleybuses, diesel buses, commuter trains, passenger trains, hiking trails, bike paths, ferry boats to the islands off the Lake Ontario shore, and even a few divided, limited-access roads, although no new freeways have been built since 1967. In other words, Toronto has a transportation system that offers a rich variety of choices; humans can drive, ride, bike, or walk to almost any location in the metro area. As in the rest of the advanced industrial world, driving a car in Canadian cities is a travel choice, not a necessity. Only the U.S. government denies this choice to its citizens.

Over the last fifty years, the federal government has intruded in the transportation marketplace, and the interstate highway system is essentially complete, including its ruinous urban components. Automobile travel has been subsidized to such a degree that its infrastructure is largely in place, while transit infrastructure has deteriorated. Huge, catch-up federal subsidies for transit would lack political support and simply perpetuate the inherent inefficiencies of subsidization, but other steps can be taken to prevent U.S. transport policies from further diminishing our cities and our national economy.

City Grid: Cure for Congestion

Traffic engineer Rick Chelman was hired to compare the potential traffic impact for two sites competing for a federal building in Portsmouth, New Hampshire. One site was adjacent to Interstate 95 on the western edge of town; the other site was in the city center.

Chelman estimated traffic congestion for both locations and determined that the I-95 site would generate 50 percent more congestion. Why? The short answer is that the street grid disperses traffic while the limited-access highway concentrates it. The grid's dispersal of traffic can be explained by the simple fact that it provides more choices.

Imagine that your workday at the federal office building is over and you are now heading home, about to enter the intersection in front of your office building. You can drive east, west, north, or south. Once you've chosen your direction, you'll have to choose again at the next intersection and at the next and so on. Theoretically, the number of available choices grows geometrically with each block—from 4 to 16 to 256. Each employee chooses from among these options.

Now imagine that your office is located on a feeder road next to the interstate. The typical suburban office park provides one dead-end access road to one feeder road to one freeway. Instead of spreading traffic, the suburban office park concentrates it.

Chelman is now coauthoring a traffic-planning manual for the Institute of Transportation Engineers (ITF), a professional organization. The manual will discuss the comparative advantages of the grid in absorbing and reducing congestion. It will explain to engineers and engineering students that traditional cities relieve traffic congestion and that the dense and complicated street patterns of older cities have not only an aesthetic value, but a practical value as well.

Until recently, traffic planning in the latter half of the twentieth century has focused on the strategy of relieving congestion by widening the path of traffic. If two lanes fill up, build four. If four won't do the trick, try eight. A secondary strategy was to bypass congestion by building roads around or separate from other streets. Both strategies move traffic faster as long as traffic remains constant. But it doesn't. Traffic quickly grows more congested as more people take shortcuts. Over the long run, the impact worsens as high-speed roads extend development, leading to longer commutes and more dependence on cars.

A similarly flawed process was conducted this century by the Army Corps of Engineers and the Bureau of Reclamation. They drained swamps and attempted to manage river basins by channeling creeks and streams and rushing runoff into a few rivers. The result in many cases has been massive flooding, such as occurred in the Pacific Northwest in early 1997. Channeling streams floods rivers. Channeling traffic floods freeways. The only difference is that the traffic rains almost every day.

Streets versus Highways

Adding lanes to solve congestion is like loosening your belt to solve obesity.

—*Walter Kulash, traffic engineer*

As superhighways were built, cities changed their streets to connect with and service the new system. Most adjacent streets were made one-way streets to accommodate on- or off-ramps. Parking was disallowed, sidewalks narrowed or eliminated, and rights-of-way expanded to speed traffic flow on and off the superhighways. Streets were, in effect, turned into ramp extensions. These changes accelerated access to the freeways but had negative side effects on downtown businesses.

Business patrons prefer convenient parking; people like to park close to the store they plan to visit. Eliminating street parking makes this difficult. In Milwaukee, we've brought back on-street parking. We've discontinued no-parking zones that allowed traffic to race through downtown toward the freeways at rush hour. Now people can park in front of the stores they want to frequent.

Wisconsin Avenue is Milwaukee's main downtown thoroughfare. Parking was banned on Wisconsin Avenue in the 1930s to allow an additional driving lane for cars. Steetcars occupied the middle lanes. After the streetcars were removed in 1957, all the lanes were devoted to auto traffic. Businesses suffered from the perception of shoppers that there was no place to park, even though a two-thousand-space parking ramp was built nearby.

Through surveys, we learned that people really wanted to have a chance to park on the avenue. So we restored on-street parking there. Now Wisconsin Avenue is lined with parked cars and the sidewalks are more often filled with people going to events, restaurants, and theaters downtown.

We've also reverted a number of one-way streets to two-way streets, making it easier for people to get around and making more efficient use of the street grid. One-way streets tend to force drivers out of their way. Two-way streets are more convenient for the people who live and conduct commerce downtown.

ISTEA

First aid for cities—a meaningful critique of, and remedy from, U.S. transportation policy—began in 1991. Senator Daniel Patrick Moynihan of New York, who understands cities better than any of his colleagues, used his power to pass legislation called the Intermodal Surface Transportation Efficiency Act (ISTEA), pronounced "ice tea." ISTEA has provided more than $152 billion to states over six years. Of that amount, $80 billion was newly flexible, that is, rather than being funneled directly into superhighway building, it could be used by state and local governments for any of a variety of programs or projects. ISTEA also allows for more local control and requires public participation in setting transportation priorities.

The jury is still out on the effectiveness of ISTEA in setting a new course for national transportation policy. The federal money is still perceived as free by states, which skews the prioritization process. After all, it's easy to buy things you don't need with money you don't earn. Also, cities are at a disadvantage in the planning process. Metropolitan planning organizations (MPOs) have been created to set regional priorities for the new federal money. Although intended to promote regional cooperation, some MPOs operate in gross violation of proportional representation. Often regional planning commissions use a one-county, one-vote process that disempowers urban populations. Both Chicago and Milwaukee, for example, suffer under systems that overwhelmingly favor the suburban population.

Still, there have been some success stories under ISTEA over the last few years. Bike trails, carpooling incentives, and traffic-calming projects are some of the ISTEA-funded alternatives that have helped cities. A group of cities interested in rail transit—including Portland, Oregon, St. Louis, Missouri, Baltimore, Salt Lake City, and Milwaukee—has formed a New Start working group to pool resources, support ISTEA, and keep rail on the federal front burner. Salt Lake City's first light-rail line has been approved, and St. Louis received a commitment from the Clinton administration for $295 million for a new leg on its rail-transit line.

St. Louis's rail-transit system was born after a long and difficult labor. The proposal was opposed loudly by many suburban officials, ridiculed by local talk-radio hosts, and condemned by the anti-transit Missouri Department of Transportation and others. But through the persistence of U.S. Congressman Dick Gephardt and former St. Louis mayor Vince Schoemehl, the rail-transit line was completed, linking downtown St. Louis with its airport and with East St. Louis, Illinois. Once people tried it, they loved it. Seventy percent of the St. Louis rail riders are brand-new transit riders. Bus ridership, instead of going down, has increased. Several suburbs that opposed the original system are now asking to be included in the new link approved and funded under ISTEA. Two suburban counties in Illinois have voted by about a two-to-one margin to tax themselves in order to get the next extension of the rail-transit system from East St. Louis to Scott Air Base in Belleville, Illinois.

Other ISTEA successes have been less quantifiable, but equally dramatic in shifting thinking in this country on transport issues. Kansas City, Missouri, citizens and local government officials, aided by the enhanced public participation provisions of ISTEA, voted down a planned limited-access beltway around the city. Atlanta officials dramatically scaled back a federally designated limited-access beltway, noting that it would do nothing to relieve congestion.

One of the least publicized parts of ISTEA has the most potential. It allows states to use some of their highway funding as seed money to develop new private highways and stimulate private financing for rebuilding and modernizing existing roads. In other words, it gives states money to explore a free-market transportation system.

If All Else Fails, Defederalize

ISTEA may be the best and last chance to define a productive role for the federal government in surface transportation. If ISTEA fails, then the focus should shift to removing the federal government from surface transportation.

Defederalizing our transportation system would help transit compete with the automobile. It wouldn't simply diminish huge federal auto subsidies; it would also force transit to provide a better product. Of course, defederalization is not likely to be absolute. Politics often restrains reform and change. Yet given the rural and suburban

THE WEALTH OF CITIES

sympathies of Congress, a reduced federal role would be, on balance, good news for transit and for cities.

I walked into Union Station near downtown Los Angeles a few years ago. On each side of me were dozens of booths used by the Southern Pacific Railroad, the Santa Fe Railroad, and all the other railroads that served Union Station before Amtrak was formed. It was much like an airline terminal, with many different private carriers in competition at a common site.

For air travel the federal government has struck a good balance between federal assistance and private competition. The federal government provides air-traffic-control services for routes of travel; the federal, state, and local governments provide the takeoff and landing platform; and the airlines provide the planes, pilots, and service. On this basis, the airlines compete. For passenger-rail travel, the federal government has set up a socialized system that confounds competition. Only one vendor, Amtrak, is allowed to participate. I enjoy riding Amtrak, but the monopolistic structure stunts its quality. Its dependence on federal subsidy for capital and on freight-rail companies for access to rights-of-way limits its ability to improve. The public has reacted by reducing its use of railroads and choosing airlines instead.

Airplanes, of course, have a huge speed advantage at distances above 350 miles, and would likely retain that market no matter how good the rail system was, but a high-quality, high-speed rail network could compete with airlines on moderate-length trips. Trains have the advantages of timeliness, all-weather travel, and center-city stations that reduce predeparture and postarrival commutes. Nearly half the departures from Chicago's O'Hare Airport are for trips of less than 250 miles, which are ripe for rail competition. The federal government could help spur that competition by treating trains as planes.

Meanwhile, as do cities, transit needs to stop whining about injustice, and learn to compete within the limited and unfair frame-

U . S . A u t o b a h n s

work allowed by the federal government. Transit can't compete by convincing the government to feel sorry for it. Instead, it needs to develop a choice that consumers will prefer, at least for some of their trips. The St. Louis light-rail system has done just that. It provides a satisfying and superior alternative to riding in a car along its route. From the airport to downtown, St. Louis transit riders encounter no traffic jams, travel at fifty or sixty miles per hour, and can read or rest during their trip. They pay one dollar instead of the twenty or twenty-five dollars it costs to take a cab. This option is particularly attractive for conventioneers, commuters, and people heading downtown for events or entertainment. Well-designed transit systems attract riders not because people feel obligated, but because they feel satisfied, even delighted, to ride it.

To rebuild our cities with new transportation programs we must replace current anti-urban policies with policies that are pro-city, or at least neutral. We need to invest existing transportation dollars in urban systems, build new rail systems, improve the old ones, and greatly increase the number and speed of trains running between large cities. Transportation policy should reinforce the natural advantage and basic strength of cities by helping people and businesses locate conveniently close to each other.

ISTEA is a step in the right direction. Further leadership is required as ISTEA is reauthorized to make sure that the highway lobby does not bend the newly flexible state and regional governments to further subsidization of the automobile-dependent lifestyle. If cities fail to get their fair share of ISTEA dollars, urban interests should remove the federal government from transportation funding altogether. Defederalizing U.S. transportation policy would help roads and transit compete on a level playing field for the first time in fifty years. Meanwhile, cities are not without options. Within the margin allowed them, they can implement transportation policies that add value and accommodate people and commerce, not just vehicles.

C H A P T E R   T E N

The New Urbanism

IN ALMOST ANY metropolitan area in the country, the local news begins with an aerial view of the downtown skyline. Why? Simply because the downtown is the most striking visual aspect of a city. Imagine starting the news each night with an image of a suburban strip mall and its parking lot. The downtown provides focus and context and helps define the metropolitan community. Celebrations, charity races, parades, and festivals—incongruous in malls or edge cities—are usually held downtown. When the New York Islanders won the Stanley Cup, their celebratory motorcade drove around and around the Nassau Coliseum parking lot; they had nowhere else to hold a parade, despite the population of over a million people in Nassau County.

Even organizations and businesses that have left the downtown often return to identify themselves with public events such as parades or charity runs. Over the past twenty years, nine of ten hospitals associated with the Milwaukee Medical College have abandoned a neighborhood just west of downtown. Most moved to a location along the beltway, with neither identity nor name. The hospital exodus brought economic depression to the neighborhood. Almost half the jobs in that area were in hospitals or related businesses, such as flower shops, religious bookstores, and restaurants. Since the county spent millions of dollars to relocate the hospitals, the taxpayers in the neighborhood experienced the added indignity of helping to pay for the rope that hanged them.

One of the last hospitals to move to the beltway was Children's Hospital. Every year Children's Hospital raises money through Al's

Run, an eight-kilometer race that draws about fifteen thousand participants. Al's Run is named for Al McGuire, former Marquette University basketball coach who took his team to the NCAA title in 1977. Marquette is the remaining anchor in the neighborhood abandoned by the medical college.

Although Children's Hospital moved in 1990, it still holds Al's Run downtown. Run organizers realize that the participants enjoy running through city streets lined with buildings of various styles and with idiosyncracies unique to Milwaukee. The course passes the twenty-story Wisconsin Gas Company building, one of Milwaukee's art deco skyscrapers. Atop the building is a beacon whose color reflects the weather conditions of the moment: warmer (red), colder (gold), no change (blue). People remember that when the flame is gold, the weather is cold, because when it's cold the gas company makes gold.

As many downtown buildings have clocks, runners can check their times by glancing at City Hall, or St. Mary's Church, or St. John Cathedral. If they're measuring their pace in five- or ten-minute increments, they can glance south, across the Menomonee valley; the huge Allen-Bradley clock tower will let them know how slow they are. The Polish Moon, as it is called by some, is the largest, four-faced electric clock in the world.

Of course, we want downtown Milwaukee to continue hosting Al's Run. It's a great cause that raises money for children. But what if we didn't? What if Al's Run had to start and end at the Children's Hospital parking lot near the beltway? Would fifteen thousand people willingly run among the strip malls and parking lots? Would art deco buildings and historic clock towers greet the runners anywhere along the route? Or would they have to be satisfied with Taco Bell and Golden Arches?

The Postcard Test

Postcards depict a city's landmarks. Cable cars, the Statue of Liberty, the Eiffel Tower, the Wrigley Building instantly identify their respective cities. Postcards also feature the beautiful images of a city.

I use slides to illustrate a speech I often give on urban design. The show juxtaposes slides of traditional urban design with slides of suburban sprawl.

"Would you put this on a postcard?" I ask my audience, whether architects, planners, civic leaders, or community activists. "If the answer is no," I caution, "why build it that way?" And yet, almost everything built these days is built in the suburban style. When people view direct comparisons of traditional urban design with sprawl, they inevitably prefer the traditional forms.

Traditional does not necessarily mean old-fashioned. Modern-style buildings can be organized in a way that pleases. The Dizengoff of Tel Aviv and Collins Avenue in Miami Beach, Florida, are lively, attractive places, lined with International Style, modern buildings.

What repels is the giant parking lots positioned in front of buildings, the pylon signs, the lack of sidewalks, the disorienting jumble that constitutes much of the postwar suburban style.

A Brief History of Ugliness

Thomas Wolfe's *From Bauhaus to Our House* describes a series of accidents that led to the way the nation looks today with its strip malls, single-family houses on cul-de-sacs, churches that resemble factories, and office parks of unadorned glass-and-steel structures. This sterile look, which has become associated with the United States, did not exist before World War II.

The dada movement started in Romania during World War I. The dada school in art—minimalist, bohemian, industrial, and antiwar—moved quickly across artistic media. In architecture it helped inspire the Bauhaus movement. Bauhaus-designed houses and apartments looked like factories. These homes for workers reflected a socialist ideal that industrial workers should live in the realm of mass production. People considered this style unattractive, however, and it died out after a few buildings were constructed.

As the Bauhaus movement was dying out in Europe, the Nazi regime came to power in 1933 and started persecuting, among others, the artists, architects, and bohemians from whom the movement arose. Many fled, some to the United States.

Austrian Mies van der Rohe became head of the Architecture School at the Illinois Institute of Technology (IIT). Walter Gropius came from Germany to Harvard. Various disciples of the French Swiss designer Le Corbusier emigrated to the United States as well. Although few of his projects were actually built, Le Corbusier had perhaps the most significant influence on American design despite the unpopularity of his workers' apartments in Europe. Yet when choosing his own home, Le Corbusier preferred the narrow streets of the artists' colony of Montmartre in Paris.

The European expatriates created the minimalist architecture of today. What was a five-year fad in Europe ended up a fifty-year trend in the United States. Rem Koolhaas is the latest guru of this style. He defends what a *Time* magazine article referred to as "McArchitecture" and takes pride in a willingness to use "extremely cheap materials" even when his clients can afford better. At the expensive Villa Dall'Ava outside Paris, "the architect . . . used orange plastic webbing, familiar from construction sites, for a balustrade on the roof." Neighbors of the Villa fought construction of the design "all the way to the French supreme court."

Frank Lloyd Wright's work was influenced by Le Corbusier. Although Wright never subscribed to Le Corbusier's theories, he did respond to them. In *City Life,* architect Witold Rybczynski notes that Wright began designing his Broadacre City, his "answer to Le Corbusier," in the mid-1930s. "Instead of concentrating people in apartment blocks, Broadacre dispersed them in individual houses on one-acre lots." People would interact with each other via a multi-level road system or some sort of individual propulsion units like 1930s visions of jet packs.

Broadacre City was not well received by architectural critics. It was considered "an embarrassing foible of an aging master." Embarrass-

The New Urbanism

ing perhaps, but much of Broadacre City exists in the development patterns of today. Although jet packs haven't yet made it, super-highways run through cities; and the large-lot, single-family home Wright designed has proven more lasting than the workers' high-rise of Le Corbusier.

A Tale of Two Streets

Kinnickinnic Avenue extends through Milwaukee's close-knit Bayview neighborhood. Old maps of Milwaukee show Kinnickinnic as one of the first routes to the city from the south. Eventually a double-track streetcar line was laid along the avenue. As the area became urbanized, city engineers established a street-grid system that encompassed Kinnickinnic and its local lanes and byways. By the turn of the century, Kinnickinnic Avenue had become the downtown of Bayview, lined with shops, offices, and apartments.

Blue Mound Road shoots straight west out of town toward the tiny town of Blue Mound, Wisconsin, located more than a hundred miles to the west. In the late 1800s Milwaukee foundries depended heavily on sand quarried from the hills around Blue Mound. Ton after ton of sand was hauled into Milwaukee along the Blue Mound Road.

Today Blue Mound Road traverses with the dignity of Dr. Jekyll the cities of Milwaukee and Wauwatosa as a predominantly urban and often residential street; once it hits the suburb of Brookfield, however, it turns into Mr. Hyde. It becomes an eight-lane, divided arterial that serves as Brookfield's main retail strip and de facto downtown. Blue Mound Road in Brookfield is among the most congested in southeastern Wisconsin. It's a booming area where people spend money at the chain malls, but it's also a place with no sidewalks, where travel is exclusively by automobile.

On Kinnickinnic Avenue, known locally as KK, the family-owned shops are doing well, too. There are almost no vacant storefronts. Crime is rare along KK. The Bayview library on KK is among the most popular in the city. The neighborhood is a clean and friendly place.

On Blue Mound Road, shops and businesses squat behind acres of parking. The buildings themselves are so insignificant that they have to be identified by pylon signs that motorists can read as they speed past—or crawl past. Wide as it is, Blue Mound Road is virtually the only means of access to establishments along the gridless commercial strip; intersecting roads come only at half-mile increments. With all traffic funneled onto one street, it is not only more congested than any other commercial area in Milwaukee, but it is also dangerous. Nothing about Blue Mound Road tells you where you are, orients you to any prevailing culture, or gives you any sense of place. The only hint that you are in Wisconsin rather than in Florida is the salt stains in the parking lots.

Kinnickinnic Avenue is fifty feet wide, bordered by eight-foot sidewalks on each side. Streets aren't built like that anymore, but until forty years ago, fifty feet was a common width for a commercial street. It works well. A lane and a half of traffic can move in either direction, cars can park on the street, and motorists have enough room to slip around double-parked cars. KK is wide enough to allow for traffic flow, narrow enough to encourage pedestrian crossings. The buildings that face each other across a fifty-foot street aren't spatially or architecturally divorced from one another. They work together across that span to create a sense of connection.

The fifty-foot commercial street was created with incredible uniformity in the United States from the time of the Civil War until the advent of World War II. It was the happy result of administrative convenience. Surveyors in the 1800s used the rod as their standard measure. A rod is sixteen and a half feet. In laying out streets, one rod in each direction was considered too narrow, and three rods seemed too wide. So engineers used the "two-rod road," and it didn't disappoint them. Sixty-six feet of right-of-way allowed eight feet of sidewalk on each side for pedestrians, ten feet in the middle of the street for the streetcar, and two ten-foot lanes in each direction—one

The New Urbanism

for parked carriages and one for traffic. As automobiles replaced carriages and streetcars, the proportions of the two-rod road adapted admirably.

The shops along KK abut the sidewalk. There is no setback. Motorists don't need pylon signs to identify the establishments they are passing along KK. They can look at the signs on the buildings or right in the shop windows and see for themselves.

And the motorists have leisure to look. They are neither rocketing past at fifty miles an hour, nor riding the brake and checking the mirrors in bumper-to-bumper traffic. Traffic moves smoothly even at rush hour. KK has short blocks and is nestled in a convenient grid. If the street seems too congested, motorists can easily switch to a parallel route a few blocks away.

KK is a pleasant place to walk. Your destination may be the hardware store, but on the way you just might take the time to stick your head in the door and say hello at Pankow's barbershop or catch a cold beer at hundred-year-old Kneisler's White House tavern.

Most buildings along KK are simple, with retail on the first floor and apartments above. Some, like Kneisler's, are spectacular, but most are modest. There are brightly painted, flat-roofed clapboard affairs; others feature Victorian embellishments; still others have adopted the Milwaukee bungalow style. Together these buildings create a street that still reflects much of the scale and character of its nineteenth-century village origins. At well over a hundred years old and counting, Kinnickinnic Avenue holds its value.

The Rise and Fall of the Mediocre U.S. Suburb

As Kinnickinnic Avenue flourishes, the Blue Mound Roads of the world may collapse under the weight of their own monotony. In his attack on the malling of the United States, *The Geography of Nowhere*, James Howard Kunstler predicts the decline of the strip-mall economy and affirms the value of cities. He writes of the suburban public realm comprising mainly roads, "The present arrangement has certainly done away with sacred places of casual public assembly, and places of repose." Kunstler's proposed solutions: traditional urban design and restoration of transit. He realizes that many people will always live in suburbs and make use of cars, but he believes that such a lifestyle should be their choice and not forced on them, that automobiles should be a convenience, not a necessity.

As popular as strip malls are, their luster is fading. Auto-oriented strip development is becoming ragged, boring, and inconvenient not only for traditional low- and middle-income urban dwellers, but also for suburbanites with money. Even teenagers are tiring of the malls. A May 1, 1996, cover story in *USA Today* begins, "The future of retailing in America may all come down to where [eighteen-year-old] Jessica Pfeifer shops. There's one place it's not: the mall. Anyplace *but* the mall." The article cites surveys that show a 22 percent drop over the last three years in teenagers who "said it was cool to hang out at the local mall" and describes the scramble by cutting-edge retailers to create antimall environments.

The small-town main street is one such environment, and it doesn't need to be created. Through thick and thin—mostly thin over the last forty years—it has survived. Now Main Street is coming back.

Cedarburg is a town of 10,086 people in the Milwaukee metropolitan area. Like Kinnickinnic Avenue, Cedarburg's main street is fifty feet wide with sidewalks on each side. Buildings relate to each other in a way that creates a sense of destination and community. Surrounding megamalls and strip development haven't hurt Cedarburg much. Its specialty shops and other commercial enterprises do well all year long.

Cedarburg isn't a typical small town; it accesses the money of a major metropolitan area. But more remote small towns are successfully resurrecting their main streets as well. *Governing* magazine's May 1996 cover story chronicles the rebirth of several small-town main streets in Oklahoma. It attributes the trend to several factors, including the declining popularity of malls. "All told in America, shopping mall vacancies now amount to the equivalent of 3,000 en-

The New Urbanism

tire medium-sized malls. . . . Mall shopping hours nationally have been declining steadily since the 1980s." The article notes that mall anchors, megastores, are beginning to opt for stand-alone locations, leaving smaller mall proprietors adrift in an empty sea of tropical plants, fountains, and Muzak, and questions whether stores will "abandon the fading strip mall for a return to Main Street, where the traffic is gradually increasing?"

An urban advantage has emerged since the publication of Garreau's *Edge City* in 1991. Edge cities are getting a little frayed around the edges. The enclosed megamall seems dated. People are rediscovering the attractiveness of Main Street, U.S.A., and choosing the urban form. National chains such as the Gap and Urban Outfitters prefer urban settings to strip sprawl. Some malls, such as those in Mashpee, Massachusetts, and Nassau County, New York, have been redesigned into urban forms by the addition of streets, sidewalks, and buildings with parking hidden behind. If cities continue to become safer, this trend should endure.

In Milwaukee we're finding that old, traditional neighborhoods near the lake or near downtown, for instance, the East Side and Bayview, are becoming more attractive to people with discretionary income. Escalating real-estate prices indicate that people who have money are increasingly drawn to the best of urban life; they've grown tired of the cul-de-sacs, isolation, and sterility of edge cities.

In a recent series on the once-chic L.A. suburbs of Antelope Valley, the *Los Angeles Times* noted:

Commuters spend up to five hours a day behind the wheel. Their children sometimes are forced to endure 12 or 13 straight hours in day care. Some teenagers, home alone for long stretches after school, are helping fuel a surge in gangs and a 26% jump last year in arrests for violent juvenile crimes. . . .

. . . like a mirage, the sizzling boom in the desert has vanished, raising pointed questions among planning experts and family counselors about whether the region's sprawling development was ill-conceived.

It's early in the game. A lot of dissatisfied suburbanites may not yet be able to articulate just what it is they want. A recent issue of *Consumer Reports* tried to do it for them. The May 1996 magazine offered advice about choosing a neighborhood in an article entitled "Neighborhoods Reborn: After a Half-Century Hiatus, Environmental and Traffic Concerns Are Bringing Back Old-Style Neighborhoods." This unprecedented move tells us that a major U.S. trend watcher sees a collective consciousness developing about the term *neighborhood*. It tells us that people are now beginning to make conscious choices about where they want to live based on how that location works, not as a cocoon or an estate or an access point to the freeway, but as a neighborhood that connects them to a richer life.

The article views as positive the notion of the "1920s style homes—in traditional neighborhoods," and identifies a return to choice among home buyers. Of course, people have enjoyed choice all along in deciding how many bedrooms, baths, and garage doors they want, but now people are beginning to respond to the opportunity to choose the physical layout of the neighborhood.

Fighting Back

Some of those who express dissatisfaction with the state of the postwar-built landscape in the United States are called new urbanists. The Congress for New Urbanism (CNU) was founded in 1993 to "restore existing urban centers and towns within coherent metropolitan regions, reconfigure the sprawling suburbs into communities of real neighborhoods and diverse districts, conserve natural environments and preserve our built legacy."

CNU was inspired by writer and activist Jane Jacobs, the first person to resist in any meaningful way the decline of traditional American design. The vision and energy for the organization derive from its founders, architects and town planners Andres Duany and

The New Urbanism

Elizabeth Plater-Zyberk of Miami, Florida, Peter Calthorpe and Dan Solomon of San Francisco, and Elizabeth Moule and Stefanos Polyzoides of Los Angeles.

The organization began as a group of renegade traditionalist architects, but quickly extended its sphere to engineers, elected officials, urban planners, bureaucrats, environmentalists, developers, and, most important, investors.

Architects and planners have rushed to join CNU, driven in part by guilt over their part in producing edge cities and in part by an intense desire to change the direction of development in the United States. A June 1, 1996, article in the *New York Times* called the CNU a movement reacting to postwar modernism, "the only organized nationwide movement of consequence by baby-boom architects."

CNU meetings are packed. At a recent convention in Charleston, South Carolina, three hundred of the CNU's sixteen hundred members strategized about how to change local zoning policies, reduce sprawl, and oppose the anticity development that has dominated in the United States for the last fifty years.

Designing for Community

Author Philip Langdon believes that neotraditional development can respond to popular demand by helping restore a sense of community:

> *What are the key precepts of the new traditionalist community? Above all, a belief in the importance of the public realm—streets, sidewalks, parks, and gathering places. In a well-conceived traditional community, the individual buildings work together to form coherent public spaces where people see and talk to one another.*

Cul-de-sac development restricts neighborly contact to the confines of dead-end streets. Traditional urban residential design offers a number of important features that reinforce the notion of community.

Sidewalks

Sidewalks are fast disappearing from the U.S. landscape. The percentage of homes with sidewalks is declining, since most new subdivisions don't have sidewalks. Eventually, sidewalks may become a historical relic. This trend is unfortunate. Children need sidewalks; elderly people use them; even people who usually drive occasionally enjoy walking on sidewalks.

Cul-de-sac suburbia can boast of its greenways and jogging paths, but these are pretty flimsy substitutes for sidewalks. If sidewalks are the bones and connective tissue of a neighborhood, suburbia suffers from rickets. Not enough vitamin C—community.

Read Jane Jacobs's 1961 masterpiece *The Death and Life of Great American Cities* and you'll find three chapters devoted to the importance of sidewalks in community life. Thirty years later, Joel Garreau's paean to deurbanization, *Edge City*, doesn't even reference the term *sidewalk* in the index. But not all modern thinkers have relegated sidewalks to the scrap heap. Far from it. Here's what *American Enterprise* editor in chief Karl Zinsmeister has to say:

> A sidewalk gives you the permission, and opportunity, to place yourself pretty close to other people in their most intimate sanctums— their yards and gardens, their front parlors, the stoops and porches where they read their newspapers on warm evenings. . . . A neighborhood where all the homes are laced together by an open footpath is a very different place than a neighborhood of houses reached only by private driveways.

Porches

On front porches our public and private lives can gracefully mingle. Sitting on a front porch we are home, with all its attendant benefits, including a modicum of privacy, yet we are simultaneously offering ourselves as a participant, passive or active by choice, in the public scene. We can quietly observe passersby as well as other porch sitters, or we can wave at them, or call to them, or invite them over, or ignore them altogether. On the porch, the option is ours.

Most traditional urban homes have front porches. Homes in cul-de-sac suburbia typically don't. They may have concrete stoops where a person can sit, waiting for someone to drive up and stick a newspaper in the tube at the end of the driveway. They may have ornamental imitations of front porches that are not even deep enough for people to sit down without bumping their knees. But they don't have porches where people are expected to sit.

One reason for the small number of front porches in cul-de-sac suburbia is that there's nothing to see from them except lawns and garage doors. There are no children playing on the sidewalks; there are no sidewalks, in fact. There are few joggers, walkers, or bicyclists passing by. There is no community life in which residents can participate simply by seeing or being seen. People enjoy this privacy, but they can feel alone. They fear strangers, but they miss the community of friends, acquaintances, and other citizens. In suburbia, the only public place where people can sit or stand is in the malls.

Suburban subdivisions have backyard patios, but the scope of the backyards is limited by private ownership. From their back patios, people don't see neighbors walking by or teenagers from down the street driving off to the movies; they don't have the chance to cheer the flagging participants in a local fund-raising run. And a child's lemonade stand won't make much money on a back patio.

The Keeper of the Flame

Since World War II, Main Street—the two-rod-wide street that has stores with sidewalks in front and apartments or offices above—has been newly constructed in only a few places; two of those places are

Disneyland and Disneyworld. Walt Disney understood, perhaps better than anyone else, American dreams and desires.

When you walk through the front gate of Disneyworld you don't see a strip mall. You see Main Street. Buildings conform strictly in line. Retail shops occupy the street level and replica apartments or offices are above. Wide sidewalks accommodate pedestrians who enjoy browsing along the big shop windows. The street is a near-exact replica of the two-rod street.

Disney bet that people from Naperville, Illinois, Levittown, New York, and Minnetonka, Minnesota, would flee the strip malls, travel thousands of miles, and spend billions of dollars to experience Main Street. His bet paid off.

Architect Witold Rybczynski, discussing the newest element to be added to Disneyworld, commented that Disney CEO Michael Eisner had "determined that it was finally time to implement Walt's vision" and build a real town. The town of 2000, Celebration, currently under construction adjacent to Disneyworld, is being built with traditional design.

You would look in vain for manifestations of the current vogues in high-fashion architecture. There is no free-form deconstructivism here, no corrugated-metal high tech. Instead, there are gable roofs with dormers, bay windows and porches, balustrades and columns.

Celebration also features a traditional main street, with three-story commercial buildings close to the street, and residential areas, with houses built close together and trees for shade. Celebration is so popular that homeowners are being chosen from a waiting list via lottery.

Nostalgia is only part of Disney's popularity. People realize, on some level, that traditional forms work. And that's what is important for cities—not hailing back to some amber-hued days of a nostalgic past, but resurrecting what works. It works in Cedarburg, Wisconsin; in Milwaukee's urban village on Kinnickinnic Avenue; on Chicago's

The New Urbanism

Devon Avenue; in Ponca City, Oklahoma; in Greenwich Village, New York; in thousands of downtowns and urban neighborhoods around the country. Visitors to Disneyworld would do well to remember this. They just might find what they are looking for—with free admission—if they search a little closer to home.

Charleston

Mayor Joe Riley of Charleston, South Carolina, was elected twenty-four years ago, at a time when the people of Charleston were trying to decide whether to preserve history as reflected in architecture or to tear the city down and modernize. When Riley, a successful realtor and ardent historic preservationist, was elected, the issue was decided.

Riley led Charleston to build on its strengths and uniqueness as a city, using historic preservation as a formula for success. Old Charleston, built mostly in the eighteenth century, was constructed on a tight grid of streets and alleys. Houses and apartments there vary in size and cost. People with money choose to live in downtown Charleston; people without money choose to live there too. They may live above a garage or in a back cottage, but poor people live together with rich people in downtown Charleston.

Charleston has become a destination city by preserving its design. It thrives at a time of reduced federal aid to cities in general and to Charleston in particular. From the 1950s through the 1970s, South Carolina representative L. Mendel Rivers chaired the House Armed Services Committee and used his power to concentrate military jobs in Charleston. With the end of Rivers's career and the eventual end of the cold war, the military pot dried up. Yet because Charleston had preserved its beauty, it could build its tourism industry.

Learning from the Suburbs

Historic preservation is a good strategy, but by itself is not enough. Cities need to study what makes suburbs attractive and adopt some of those characteristics without sacrificing the elements that attract people to urban environments in the first place.

There is a lot to learn. I toured new homes with Vince Kuttemperoor, a successful suburban-home developer. I was impressed, not so much with where the homes were located, but with the homes themselves. They were of the highest quality and met the latest consumer desires. These homes were the first in the Milwaukee area with work space in the middle of kitchens, wood floors in kitchens, solariums opening off kitchens, exercise rooms with floor-to-ceiling windows, and large, walk-in closets. Thirty years ago developers featured master bedrooms. Now they feature master bathrooms. A thousand years from now, archaeologists may wonder at our priorities. In the meantime, smart developers such as Kuttemperoor are discerning them and delivering the product.

Developers and redevelopers in cities must respond to consumer tastes as well. They can't take the attitude that people should live in the city because it's the right thing to do, nor can they pin their hopes strictly on historical appeal. City homes need the amenities people want. The good news is that Kuttemperoor is planning an urban development in Milwaukee.

Central business districts also need to study their suburban counterparts. They need to learn from suburban industrial parks and market their advantages. As Garreau has pointed out, suburbs don't have sidewalks, they have jogging paths, and in suburban corporate parks access to jogging paths is an important amenity.

Well, cities have jogging paths too. In older U.S. cities miles and miles of sidewalks as well as jogging and walking paths connect the downtowns with natural features such as rivers and lakes or beautiful parks, many of which were designed by planners such as Frederick Law Olmsted, John Nolen, and Daniel Burnham. These city paths are usually more interesting and more pleasing than are the jogging paths that wind through some contrived environment of artificial berms in corporate parks.

The New Urbanism

Movie theaters are another amenity of suburban corporate parks. Cities can compete by locating multiscreen theaters downtown. Former basketball star Magic Johnson opened a theater complex in the Watts section of Los Angeles and now has a successful chain of theaters in African American neighborhoods across the United States.

Health clubs are a key feature near suburban executive parks. The martini lunch has been replaced by the aerobics, swimming, hoops, or Nautilus lunch. Cities should encourage full-facility health clubs to locate downtown and in traditional urban business districts. Bally's, The Athletic Club, the YMCA or YWCA are all significant boons to commerce.

Today's consumer is far different from the consumer of twenty- five years ago. Committed city advocates can say that multiplex theaters or shopping malls or jogging paths or health clubs are not important compared to all the other advantages of urban living. But many people think these features are essential. And they can be more exciting in an urban setting. Why can't people have both? If cities are going to compete, let's give people what they want.

The Best City Park in Milwaukee

One advantage that suburbs have over cities is space. They have plenty of space, but generally do little that's interesting with it. Suburbs rarely leave space alone to grow wild or create from it much more than parking lots surrounding nondescript buildings. Such space, neither urban nor rural, is what Leopold Kohr calls "the rural idiocy of the suburbs."

For people living in cities who don't have half-acre lots but who need green space, I suggest the countryside. City dwellers should visit it every so often. If they can't get out of the city, they can go to a park. Although an urban park is not likely to substitute for wide open spaces, it can provide gathering space defined by the buildings around it. The Boston Common; Rittenhouse Square, Philadelphia's most cherished park; and Cathedral Park in Milwaukee are examples of this phenomenon.

Cathedral Park occupies one small block downtown. It's a simple park—no architecture, no built environment, just trees and grass—but it's popular. Its architecture is supplied by the buildings that surround it, paid for by the private sector. These buildings are close to the street, they face the park, and their windows help connect them to the park's public activity. On one side of the park, St. John's Cathedral and its clock tower, built in 1858, serves as the focal point. Other structures can be seen behind the bordering buildings in layers that delight one's sense of proportion and style. Cathedral Park is full of activity at almost any hour, with people walking, reading, eating, or just relaxing.

Less than a mile away MacArthur Square Park sits empty. Built atop a five-level, underground parking lot, at a cost of millions of dollars, MacArthur Square Park has fountains, built-in benches, staircases, and an elaborate variety of paved surfaces, gravel, and grass all delineated by trees and bushes in concrete planting beds.

On the east a concrete wall at the park's boundary keeps people from falling among the cars entering the parking lot underneath; on the south stands the blank, concrete wall of a museum; and on the north are law-enforcement offices with windows veiled by concrete slats. The park is as unpopular as it was expensive.

Every spring, a memorial service for police officers is held at MacArthur Square and draws a large crowd to the appropriately solemn venue. However, from Memorial Day until Labor Day, MacArthur Square Park is the one park in town that always has picnic tables available.

City Hall, City Beautiful

Milwaukee City Hall was built a hundred years ago during the time of the City Beautiful movement that was led by Daniel Burnham,

The New Urbanism

Alfred Clas, Frederick Law Olmsted, and, later, John Nolen. People were trying to build in a context that would make their cities more beautiful than the cities of Europe. In some cases, they succeeded. Burnham's Wacker Drive along the Chicago River and Olmsted's Central Park added profoundly to the greatness of Chicago and New York. The architects and planners did not work alone, however. Civic leaders showed bold vision and serious purpose as well.

In Milwaukee, city aldermen held a design competition for the new city hall and specified that the design had to include an eight-story atrium. This was a conscious effort to build the City Beautiful.

Witold Rybczynski, one of the more prominent architects in the world today, visited Milwaukee in 1992 to promote his book *Home*. (He has since written *City Life*). During his visit, he toured the city. He made some critical comments, as architects do when they visit cities and view the work of other architects. The last stop on his tour was City Hall.

Later, when he addressed the Milwaukee Literary Society, he said, "You have the most beautiful City Hall in the world."

"In the world?" I asked.

"Yes," he said, "Not just in the United States. In the world."

After he left, I thought about the people who built U.S. cities a hundred years ago. As they entered a new century, they aspired not merely to build functional structures, but to build with purpose for people and posterity, to assemble buildings in a way that would delight their citizens and emblematize the good life of the city. And with New York's Public Library, Cleveland's Terminal Building, Milwaukee's City Hall, and scores of others, they succeeded.

Now, as we enter the next millennium, it's time to raise our sights. It's time to understand what has been done to U.S. cities and suburbs in the last fifty years. It's time to do better.

CHAPTER ELEVEN

Lessons in Civic Life

AT THE END OF WORLD WAR II cities suddenly became expendable. Communities with porches, sidewalks, streets, blocks, neighborhoods, and grand public spaces were largely abandoned and replaced with the now-familiar collection of strips, cul-de-sacs, and sprawl. But it wasn't only design that hurt U.S. cities. As the cities deteriorated physically they also lost their sense of purpose. The dynamic urban markets that drove commerce and served as the ladder to prosperity for millions of immigrants in the nineteenth and early twentieth centuries began to be viewed as the problem, even the cause, of poverty. The city as incurable disease replaced the city as platform for opportunity. Remedies intended to revitalize instead overwhelmed the productive assets of cities. Social services, public housing, welfare schemes, and other efforts at artificial respiration became bigger and more important than the cities and their people. Instead of being rescued, U.S. cities were victimized by federal interference, and their status as victims was institutionalized.

Ed Banfield, in *The Unheavenly City,* warned against this turn of events and argued that "the city, far from being a cause of poverty, has proved to be a remarkably efficient machine for transforming it into prosperity and even affluence."

More recently, Michael Porter, in an article entitled "The Competitive Advantage of the Inner City," argued that central cities can compete in the marketplace very well by exploiting their natural advantages. These advantages include "physical location, access to regional clusters, demand conditions, and human resources." Porter believes that central cities have tools with which to compete and must learn to use them.

One prescription for urban success is the free market. Cities are essentially *places* and *markets* more than they are government entities. State and federal interference with markets, though sometimes well-intentioned, has on balance hurt cities. Yet, as cities naturally contain most of the elements necessary for success, they can rebound and prosper despite their burdened state. Much of what is necessary to ensure urban success amounts to no more than removing baggage and setting cities free.

There are, however, some specific steps that can help U.S. cities, and the nation, become more prosperous in the twenty-first century. I sketch some of these steps, according to issue area, here, though the list is by no means exhaustive, nor does it fully summarize this book.

Three important areas are primarily the responsibility of cities themselves: budget and management, crime, and design.

- *Budget and Management* Since World War II cities have sought federal-transfer payments to solve their problems. This type of federal aid increased for a while, but is now largely nonexistent. We should leave it that way. Also, although states have a role to play in municipal and educational finances by equalizing property taxes, cities should focus more on improving productivity and less on finding more state money. Cities must recognize that it is an act of social justice to reduce the tax burden on urban taxpayers, whether the tax is local, state, or federal. Costs can be reduced through sound management techniques, in particular by building competition into the process of obtaining government services and by measuring outcomes rather than programmatic inputs. Leaner, less costly state and federal government would be a great boon to cities as well. We should not forget that city residents pay state and federal taxes. Finally, eliminating the federal deficit would reduce the future burden of federal taxes and allow urban marketplaces to be more productive.

- *Crime* Cities should substantially and permanently reduce crime. Crime chases away home owners and investors and thus devalues cities. The state and federal governments ought to be supportive of cities by effectively operating their respective criminal justice systems. States especially should stop paroling criminals into cities to repeat their offenses. The frontline responsibility for solving urban safety problems lies with the cities, however. Such cities as Charleston, South Carolina, New York, and Milwaukee have reduced crime through an attitude of absolute intolerance of crime, a will to put more police officers on the street, renewed attention to reducing quality-of-life crimes, and careful application of community policing as a tool rather than as a goal in itself.

- *Design* Suburban life, the automobile-dependent lifestyle, strip development, and shopping malls are wearing thin. The United States is ready for a return to competent planning and design. Cities will benefit from this trend. Cities that support and emphasize their urban form are increasingly appealing to people making choices about where to live and work. Cities can learn from their suburban counterparts, yet continue to foster their traditional strengths: predictable and coherent architectural rules, mixed uses, sidewalks, grid patterns, inviting public places, windows, and front porches. These simple elements make places more livable.

Some changes necessary to unleash the power of cities fall to the state and federal governments.

- *Welfare* Current welfare reforms must be changed from workfare to work. The federal government gives states money and flexibility with which to address welfare reform, but its policy is so vague that states may abuse that flexibility and support their own welfare bureaucracies. Urban welfare recipients need wage-paying jobs, not more state rules and bureaucracy. State and local governments should use their new flexibility to administer work programs according to a competitive model; that is, they should require job-placement and job-maintenance agencies, public or private, to demonstrate success. Getting people into work and keeping them there should be a prerequisite for the existence of these agencies. Replacement of welfare with work will profoundly benefit cities.

- *Education* The federal government should support parental school choice for kindergarten through grade twelve or get out of education at that level. Because of their large and diverse populations, cities should be able to provide the greatest array of educational choices and the highest-quality education when the publicly financed school monopoly is broken.

- *Housing* The federal government should get out of the housing business altogether. Federal interference in the housing market has virtually eliminated privately financed, low-cost housing and homogenized the choices available to people with low to moderate incomes. The mortgage-interest deduction should be capped so that subsidization of construction of large, suburban homes at the expense of more affordable, efficient, urban housing is gradually reduced.

- *Trade and Immigration* Trade is the primary historical underpinning of most cities. Rather than micromanage trade, the federal government should facilitate trade by safeguarding trade routes and navigation. Special-interest influence over trade policy should be recognized for what it is and eliminated. Tariffs and quotas should be abolished. Restrictions on immigration, especially for skilled and educated applicants, should be loosened. One great strength of the United States is its constant rejuvenation from the energy and new ideas of immigrants.

- *Environment* The federal government can help protect the environment by encouraging proximity. City dwellers consume far fewer resources per capita than do their suburban counterparts. Subsidies for highway building and exurban housing should be discontinued. The federal government should institute market-based measures that result in environmental protection through natural economic activity. One such measure is pollution pricing, building the true cost of production and disposal of a product into its retail price. On an international scale, sustainability should be incorporated into the official measure of economic output.

- *Transportation* The federal record on transportation is abysmal. The government should consider complete defederalization. As in Canada, transportation decisions should be made locally and regionally, using local and regional money. The eventual result would be recognition of a more cost-effective, efficient transportation system that moves people rather than just cars. Absent defederalization, state and federal governments should substantially shift their priorities from the dispersal of people exclusively via freeways so that people have travel choices.

The Value of Cities

In the twentieth century, the United States has led the world to new levels of personal freedom. Our culture and ideals have sown democracy throughout much of the world. Our technology eases the tasks of daily life, freeing time for thinking, playing, and living. Examples of our music, our food, and our version of the English

THE WEALTH OF CITIES

language can be found everywhere. And the U.S. culture and economy are gaining strength. People are embracing the information age. Our economy, more open to innovation than any other in the world, has allowed the United States to be first in software development, the Internet, web sites, and mass ownership of computers. The twentieth century has been the U.S. Century, and yet something seems to be missing.

People are seeking more from life. People are seeking a sense of belonging, of community. They may find much of what they are looking for on television or in shopping malls, but I believe part of what they are looking for can be found in real neighborhoods, in real cities.

The city, its residents, and the urban form are presently stigmatized in the United States. U.S. cities are associated with the problems of poverty, social injustice, and decay, and to make matters worse, there is an almost absolute expectation by everyone, city officials included, that cities will fail to solve these problems.

Over the years, city leaders have tried to motivate taxpayers, through the federal government, to give cities money by appealing for sympathy. They have also tried to motivate taxpayers by warning that without help, cities will explode into violence. They have told people to feel sorry for cities and to fear them. Yet feelings are not the same as solutions; pity quickly turns into contempt and fear into hatred. You can't build a city on fear and you can't build a city on pity. You can build cities on their value as a setting for commerce and culture.

The raw materials of cities—diversity, proximity, choice, community, and markets—are the ingredients of human civilization. U.S. cities, if they can solve their own problems and be freed from the problems foisted on them by a clumsy and intrusive federal government, can give Americans much of what they are looking for.

There is some evidence that the turnaround could be faster than the decline. Prosperity springs quickly from big reductions in crime in New York and Boston. Private investment follows the fiscal sta-

Lessons in Civic Life

bility achieved by Ed Rendell in Philadelphia. And hope builds in Milwaukee and Cleveland as school choice empowers parents. The payoff for efficiency, safety, and excellence is almost immediate. As people see beyond the pathology of cities and notice improvement in the quality of lives, they also begin to notice the excitement, beauty, and value of cities.

The last fifty years have been difficult, yet cities have endured. Cities are resilient; they hold more lasting value than can be destroyed in a few decades, more lasting value than is found in the thin smear of suburban development intended to replace urban life.

I believe that a second, closer look will reveal that cities, U.S. cities, have much to offer our country in the twenty-first century. In fact, I believe that the twenty-first century will be the Century of Cities, a time when the world, and particularly, the United States, will benefit from the wealth of cities.

Notes

Chapter One

page 1: The rioters killed fifty people . . .: *1993 World Almanac* (New York: Pharos Books, 1992), p. 57.

page 3: "Payne has jumped through more hoops . . .": Elizabeth Gleck, "The Impossible Dream," *Time,* 19 February 1996, p. 51.

page 3: "Some of the promised funding . . .": John R. Emshwiller, "Empty Stores Still Dot the Riot-Torn Areas of L.A.," *Wall Street Journal,* 22 May 1996.

page 4: "Instead of offering political advantages . . .": John Kass, "Dinkins Calls for NY Meeting," *Chicago Tribune,* 20 June 1990.

page 6: Civic-minded Milwaukeeans threw their support . . .: Robert W. Wells, *Yesterday's Milwaukee* (Miami: E. A. Seeman, 1976), p. 80. I am indebted to Wells for much of the information and phraseology contained in the following description of early-twentieth-century Milwaukee. See also Wells, *This Is Milwaukee* (Garden City, N.Y.: Doubleday, 1970), pp. 140–80.

page 6: "Every weekday at 6:30 A.M. . . .": Wells, *Yesterday's Milwaukee,* p. 89.

page 7: That summer Ole Evinrude . . .: Harry H. Anderson and Frederic I. Olson, *Milwaukee: At the Gathering of the Waters* (Tulsa, Okla.: Continental Heritage Press, 1991), p. 81.

page 7: The Milwaukee Road provided jobs . . .: John Gurda, *The West End, Merrill Park, Pigsville, Concordia* (Milwaukee: Milwaukee Humanities Program, University of Wisconsin-Milwaukee, 1980), p. 28.

page 7: On the near north side . . .: Eric Lucas, "Lakeside Legacy," *Midwest Express Magazine,* May/June 1996, p. 31.

page 7: "all the men do there is fish . . .": Wells, *Yesterday's Milwaukee,* p. 73.

THE WEALTH OF CITIES

page 8: Among large cities, Milwaukee was second . . .: Lucas, "Lakeside Legacy," p. 31.

page 9: "[S]omeone said, `Well gentlemen . . .'": Edward S. Kerstein, *Milwaukee's All-American Mayor* (Englewood, N.J.: Prentice-Hall, 1966), p. 135.

page 10: "commensurate with what we have . . .": Mark I. Gelfand, *A Nation of Cities* (New York and London: Oxford University Press, 1975), p. 35. Much of the following account of the USCM is taken from Gelfand, pp. 32–39.

page 10: "The Democratic mayor . . .": Ibid., p. 36.

page 10: "Curley first descended on Washington . . .": Jack Beatty, *The Rascal King* (Reading, Mass.: Addison-Wesley, 1992), p. 368.

page 11: "The crying need in America today . . .": Gelfand, *A Nation of Cities,* p. 38.

page 11: "It would be cheaper for Congress to provide a loan . . .": Ibid., p. 41.

page 11: "It was possible to see that these roads . . .": Daniel Patrick Moynihan, "ISTEA's Principal Author, Senator Moynihan, Shares Views," *U.S. Mayor,* 23 December 1996, p. 3.

page 12: "continue to exert our efforts . . .": Henry Maier, 1972 inaugural address prepared text, Milwaukee Public Library Archives.

page 12: "There is a challenge to win . . .": Henry Maier, 1984 inaugural address prepared text, Milwaukee Public Library Archives.

page 13: Naturally we were all patting each other . . .: Telephone conversation with Richard Heaps, May 1996.

page 15: "I think we are headed for . . .": George Gilder, "City vs. Country: Tom Peters and George Gilder Debate the Impact of Technology on Location," *Forbes ASAP,* 27 February 1995, p. 56.

page 17: "The many diverse elements . . .": Lewis Mumford, *The City in History* (New York: Harcourt Brace, 1961), p. 34.

page 17: "Men, thinly scattered, make a go . . .": I recall this quote, which may not be precise, from various readings on Samuel Johnson. I suspect it may come from Boswell's *Life of Samuel Johnson.*

page 20: "clusters of exuberant variety . . .": Tom Peters, "City vs. Country: Tom Peters and George Gilder Debate the Impact of Technology on Location," *Forbes ASAP,* 27 February 1995, p. 57.

page 20: "The notion that telecommunication . . .": Ibid., p. 76.

Notes

Chapter Two

page 25: "By the time 1990 rolled around . . .": W. Wilson Goode, *In Goode Faith* (Valley Forge, Pa.: Judson Press, 1992), p. 286.

page 29: "notable for the size of the . . .": Thomas Schlenker, M.D., and Kathleen Fessler, R.N., "Measles in Milwaukee," *Wisconsin Medical Journal,* July 1990, p. 405.

page 35: "People [i.e., private vendors] do treat the government . . .": Ed Rendell, "Privatization 1996" (remarks to the Reason Foundation conference, September 1995), p. 14.

page 38: "In many if not most cases . . .": Peter Drucker, "Really Reinventing Government," *Atlantic,* February 1995, p. 54.

page 44: "Norquist's law . . . is named after . . .": Michael Barone, "Government Gets a Shrink," *U.S. News and World Report,* 20 June 1994, p. 38.

Chapter Three

page 49: *Fortune* recently noted . . .: As quoted in "Criteria Change Gets Milwaukee on List," *Milwaukee Journal Sentinel,* 22 October 1996, p. 9A.

page 49: In Milwaukee over the last five years . . .: Milwaukee Police Department, "Major Crime Clearance Summary," 28 October 1996. The sexual assault statistics cover only the last four years, as a new method of measurement began in 1992.

page 50: "he alone was condemned.": William M. Bulger, *While the Music Lasts* (New York, Houghton Mifflin Company, 1996), p. 2.

page 51: "The agenda of jobs and inner-city renewal . . .": Seth Mydans, "Gangs Go Public in New Fight for Respect," *New York Times,* 2 May 1993.

page 52: "crime ranks among the most important reasons . . .": Michael E. Porter, "The Competitive Advantage of the Inner City," *Harvard Business Review,* May/June 1995, Reprint 95310, pp. 63–64.

page 56: "If Parole Stop is not implemented . . .": Fredrick Gordon, "Parole Stop Strengthens City's Attack on Crime," *Milwaukee Journal Sentinel,* 12 May 1996.

THE WEALTH OF CITIES

page 56: Keeping criminals behind bars expresses . . .: John J. Dilulio Jr., "Prisons Are a Bargain, by Any Measure," *New York Times*, 16 January 1996.

page 57: "Bratton has made sure that everyone . . .": George L. Kelling, "How to Run a Police Department," *City Journal*, Autumn 1995, p. 40.

page 60: By working systematically and assertively . . .: Ibid., p. 41.

Chapter Four

page 69: "acceded to what had been unthinkable.": Michael Wines, *New York Times*, 24 September 1995.

page 70: "Running such a system efficiently . . .": Lawrence Mead, "Growing a Smaller Welfare State," *New York Times*, 3 December 1995.

page 70: When he left office in March 1933 . . .: Arthur E. Burns and Edward A. Williams, *Federal Work, Security, and Relief Programs*, Research Monographs, Division of Research, Work Projects Administration (New York: DeCapo Press, 1971). This work of Burns and Williams is the source of all depression-era figures used in this chapter, unless otherwise noted.

page 71: "drew plans for the Civil Works Administration . . .": Robert Sherwood, *Roosevelt and Hopkins* (New York: Harper and Brothers, 1948), p. 52.

page 74: Instead, TANF punts back to the states . . .: This analysis of the federal TANF block grant is derived largely from an article by David R. Riemer, which appeared in "Viewpoint," *Planning*, November 1996.

page 78: Of the active participants, 77 percent were . . .: The New Hope Project, "Progress Report," June 1996, p. 2.

page 79: The best way to connect the unemployed poor . . .: See David R. Riemer, "Replacing Welfare with Work: The Case for an Employment Maintenance Model," *Focus*, Winter 1994/95 (University of Wisconsin-Madison Institute for Research on Poverty), pp. 23–29.

Chapter Five

page 83: "As Suburban Nests Empty . . .": Haya El Nasser, "As Suburban Nests Empty, Couples Flocking to the City," *USA Today*, 4 November 1996.

Notes

page 83: "inner-city neighborhoods can be repeopled . . .": David Rusk, *Cities without Suburbs* (Washington, D.C.: The Woodrow Wilson Center Press, 1993), p. 129.

page 85: On April 27, 1992 . . .: Daniel McGroarty provides an account of this event in *Break These Chains: The Battle for School Choice* (Rocklin, Calif.: Forum, 1996), pp. 126–29.

page 87: In each case, spending per pupil . . .: Jonathan Kozol, *Savage Inequalities* (New York: Crown Publishers, 1991).

page 91: "an instrument of distributive justice.": quoted by Peter Cookson Jr., *School Choice : The Struggle for the Soul of American Education* (New Haven and London: Yale University Press, 1984), p. 20.

page 92: A middle school cancels the final period . . .: Alan J. Borsuk, "Schools Counting on Pupils Today," *Milwaukee Journal Sentinel,* 20 September 1996, p. 1B.

page 93: Bureaucratization, for all its flaws . . .: John E. Chubb and Terry M. Moe, *Politics, Markets, and America's Schools* (Washington, D.C.: Brookings Institute, 1990), p. 12.

page 93: Goals become confused as schools are asked . . .: Ibid., p. 54.

page 94: "there is little systematic relationship . . .": Eric A. Hanushek, "Making America's Schools Work," *The Brooking Review,* Fall 1994, p. 10.

page 95: "econometric and experimental evidence shows . . .": Ibid., pp. 10–11.

page 95: "in Milwaukee, twenty-six cents of every school dollar . . .": David Harmer, *School Choice* (Washington, D.C.: Cato Institute, 1994), p. 42.

page 97: "Choice is a self-contained reform . . .": Chubb and Moe, *Politics,* p. 217.

Chapter Six

page 100: "By any realistic standard . . .": M. Carter McFarland, *Federal Government and Urban Problems* (Boulder, Colo.: Westview Press, 1978), p. 16.

page 100: Former *New York Daily News* columnist . . .: Pete Hamill, *A Drinking Life: A Memoir* (Boston: Little, Brown, 1994).

page 101: One of their creations was known as the "Polish flat.": Judith T. Kenny and Thomas C. Hubka, "City Reform versus Neighborhood Traditions: Milwaukee's Urban Reform Efforts and the Housing

Goals of the Polish Community, 1900–1920," *Research and Opinion*
(Milwaukee: Urban Research Center, University of Wisconsin-
Milwaukee, April 1996). I am indebted to Kenny and Hubka for
much of the discussion of both the Polish flat and the two-story
duplex.

page 103: "the private housing market generated . . .": Howard Huseck, "We
Don't Need Subsidized Housing," *City Journal,* Winter 1997, p. 52.

page 104: "The 12th and 14th wards are more than any others . . .": Kenny
and Hubka, "City Reform," p. 6.

page 104: "crowded houses and lots did exist . . .": Ibid.

page 105: Lot coverage restrictions gradually eliminated . . .: Ibid., p. 7.

page 105: "slums contain amenities . . .": Leopold Kohr, *The Inner City,*
(Talybont, Wales: Y Lolfa, 1989), p. 35.

page 106: The Mount Auburn cemetery in Cambridge, Massachusetts . . .:
See Garry Wills, *Lincoln at Gettysburg* (New York: Simon and
Schuster, 1992), pp. 63–73.

page 107: The first garden subdivision, Llewellyn Park . . .: Witold
Rybczynski, *City Life* (New York: Scribner, 1995), p. 180. See also
James Howard Kunstler, *The Geography of Nowhere* (New York:
Simon and Schuster, 1993), pp. 46–48.

page 107: French architect Leon Krier . . .: Lecture to Congress for New
Urbanism, Charleston, S.C., May 1996.

page 108: "this type of housing with this type of tenant . . .": McFarland,
Federal Government, p. 131.

page 109: "Where sites could be found," he wrote . . .: Ibid.

page 110: "more money per square foot has been spent . . .": Roberta Brandes
Gratz, *The Living City* (New York: Simon and Schuster, 1989), p. 18.

page 111: Unfortunately, we have made a fundamental error.: Irving
Welfeld, *HUD Scandals* (New Brunswick, N.J.: Transaction
Publishers, 1992), p. 159.

page 113: "possible for builders to plan and construct . . .": McFarland,
Federal Government, p. 118.

page 113: "not one of Levittown's 82,000 residents . . .": John A. Powell,
"Tax Policy and Racial Segregation in Housing," American Bar
Association Tax and Social Policy Forum, 2 August 1996, p. 15.

page 113: The Kerner Commission report noted that until 1949 . . .: United
States Kerner Commission, *The Kerner Report,* with introductions

Notes

by Fred R. Harris and Tom Wicker (New York, Pantheon Books, 1988), p. 474.

page 113: "a headlong rush to the cliff,": Welfeld, *HUD Scandals,* p. 29.

page 114: The expansion of FHA to existing housing . . .: Sheldon Lubar, interview with the author, January 1997.

page 115: Welfeld, *HUD Scandals,* p. 136.

page 120: "no further drug activity for a period of sixty days . . .": Milwaukee Drug Abatement Project, "Statistical Report: Numbers for entire program thru 8/6/96."

page 120: In 1994, income earners in the top 20 percent . . .: Low Income Housing Special Information Service, special memorandum, 1993.

Chapter Seven

page 124: "the city-state was always a more natural . . .": Neal R. Peirce, *Citistates,* (Washington, D.C.: Seven Locks Press, 1993), p. 6.

page 124: It is the world's largest exporter of garments . . .: See William Peterson, "Free Trade Is the Best Trading System," *Trade: Opposing Viewpoints,* ed. William Dudley (San Diego: Greenhaven Press, 1991) p. 23; and Milton Friedman, *Free to Choose* (San Diego: Harcourt Brace Jovanovich, 1991) p. 34.

page 125: Protective tariffs are as much applications of force . . .: Quoted by James Bovard in *The Fair Trade Fraud* (New York: St. Martin's Press, 1991), p. 307.

page 126: "Our trade laws routinely inflate domestic prices . . .": Bovard, "The U.S. Is Not the Victim of Unfair Trade Practices," *Trade: Opposing Viewpoints,* ed. William Dudley (San Diego: Greenhaven Press, 1991), p. 83.

page 128: "Since 1983, the U.S. has brought more unfair-trade cases . . .": Ibid., p. 79.

page 129: "Indeed," he says, "the need to meet foreign competition . . .": Friedman, *Free to Choose,* p. 46.

page 131: "for almost the entire history of the United States . . .": Bovard, *The Fair Trade Fraud,* p. 71.

page 131: According to Bovard, from 1980 to 1990 . . .: Ibid.

page 132: "The success of the United States," says Milton Friedman . . .: Friedman, *Free to Choose,* p. 37.

page 134: "If the Jones Act is the god-send . . .": Robert Quartel, "The Jones Act: Keep It or Kill It?" *Journal of Commerce,* 11 July 1996.

page 137: "City officials presented the report's findings . . .": Celia W. Dugger, "Immigrant Influence Rises in New York City in 1990s," *New York Times,* 9 January 1997.

page 138: Also, these immigrants serve as foundations . . .: U.S. Department of Housing and Urban Development, *The State of the Cities,* 1997, pp. 42–43.

Chapter Eight

page 141: assembling "100 little country manors . . .": James Howard Kunstler, "On the Road: It's Life on Long Island," *Newsday,* 16 June 1996, p. 37.

page 142: "The preservation of the environment and the avoidance of undue pollution . . .": Milton Friedman, *Free to Choose* (San Diego: Harcourt Brace Jovanovich, 1990), p. 214.

page 143: "We have simply reached the point . . .": Lester Thurow, *The Zero Sum Society* (New York: Basic Books, 1980), p. 105.

page 143: Pollution, like fraud, is something you impose on others . . .: Quoted by Frances Cairncross, *Costing the Earth* (Boston: Harvard Business School Press, 1992), p. 6.

page 146: Minnesota enacted the first brownfields program . . .: Charles D. Bader, "Remediation," *Remediation Management,* May/June 1996, p. 9.

page 147: Wichita, Kansas, for example, is waging and winning its own battle . . .: Ibid., p. 10.

page 148: "Portland has succeeded perhaps more than any other Western city . . .": Bob Ortega, "Portland Shows Nation's Planners How to Guide Growth," *Wall Street Journal,* 26 December 1995.

page 148: "Even though the Urban Growth Boundary looks permissive . . .": Carl Abbott, *Portland: Planning, Politics, and Growth in a 20th Century City* (Lincoln: University of Nebraska Press, 1983), p. 258.

page 149: In 1973, McCall succeeded in strengthening the bill . . .: Ibid., p. 251.

Notes

Chapter Nine

page 153: "When the American people, through their Congress . . .": Lewis Mumford, *The Highway and the City* (New York: Harcourt Brace Jovanovich, 1963), p. 234.

page 155: Detroit demolished 5,994 dwellings in 1995 . . .: Tim Jones, "Detroit Sees a Glimmer of Renaissance," *Chicago Tribune,* 22 November 1996.

page 156: [I]f the purpose of the motorway as now conceived . . .: Norman Bel Geddes, *Magic Motorways* (New York: Random House, 1940), p. 211.

page 157: He notes that the original suburbs . . .: See Jonathan Barnett, *The Fractured Metropolis* (New York: HarperCollins, IconEds, 1995), pp. 96–101.

page 157: Suburbanization was originally so difficult to distinguish . . .: Kenneth Schneider, *On the Nature of Cities* (San Francisco: Jossey-Bass Publishers, 1979), p. 54.

page 158: "The fatal mistake we have been making . . .": Mumford, *The Highway and the City,* p. 237.

page 158: It was Macadam who made the revolutionary proposal . . .: Sylvia Crowe, *The Landscape of Roads* (London: Architectural Press, 1960), p. 24.

page 159: "the stark realization that the automobile . . .": Schneider, *Cities,* p. 237.

page 159: "urban disorder must not be allowed . . .": Charles Glover, "The Challenge of a New Highway Program," *Highway and the Landscape,* ed. W. Brewster Snow (New Brunswick, N.J.: Rutgers University Press, 1959), p. 57.

page 159: Cleveland's inner-belt freeway, for example . . .: Richard M. Bernard, *Snow Belt Cities* (Bloomington: Indiana University Press, 1990), p. 110.

page 160: "a great, thin smear, incapable of generating . . .": Jane Jacobs, *The Death and Life of Great American Cities* (New York: Random House, 1961), p. 351.

page 161: "unplanned combinations of existing ideas": Quoted in Edward L. Glaeser, "Why Economists Still Like Cities," *City Journal,* Spring 1996, p. 75.

page 165: "It is said by our Comptroller that the automobile . . .": Daniel Hoan, inaugural address text, 15 April 1924, Milwaukee Public Library Archives.

page 165: Today about 50 percent of Milwaukee's municipal levy . . .: See Ken Kinney, "Should Property Taxes Subsidize Automobile Usage?" City of Milwaukee Strategic Planning Staff Report, March 1991.

page 166: He had spent a summer working on a road gang . . .: Robert Caro, *The Path to Power* (New York: Alfred A. Knopf, 1982), pp. 132–34.

page 168: "to achieve integrity of automobile movement . . .": Quoted in Schneider, *Cities*, p. 64.

page 170: The routes out of the city will be faster . . .: Glover, "New Highway Program," p. 69.

page 170: "Highway planning is continually hampered . . .": Joseph Ingraham, "Politics and Road Building," *Highway and the Landscape,* ed. W. Brewster Snow (New Brunswick, N.J.: Rutgers University Press, 1959), p. 178.

page 170: "It is a typical big-city situation . . .": Ibid., p. 179.

page 170: "Construction is not proceeding . . . because the highway engineers . . .": Henry Maier, Mayor's Transportation Message, draft no. 5 prepared text, Milwaukee Public Library Archives.

page 171: "Headaches are an occupational disease . . .": Henry A. Barnes, *The Man with the Red and Green Eyes* (New York: E.P. Dutton and Company, 1965), p. 13.

page 171: "We must create a new rural environment . . .": Quoted in James Sundquist, *Dispersing Population* (Washington, D.C.: Brookings Institute, 1975), p. 1.

page 171: "Population imbalance is at the core . . .": Ibid., p. 5.

page 171: "specific policy for the settlement of people . . .": Ibid.

page 171: If the people of a democratic country want a pattern . . .: Ibid., pp. 280–81.

Chapter Ten

page 181: When the New York Islanders won the Stanley Cup . . .: Claude Shostal, quoted in Bruce Lambert, "Suburban Nassau County

Notes

Makes Plans to Turn a Sprawling Center into a Focal Hub," *New York Times,* 18 January 1997.

page 183: Thomas Wolfe's *From Bauhaus to Our House* describes . . .: Thomas Wolfe, *From Bauhaus to Our House* (New York: Farrar, Straus and Giroux, 1981). Also see James Howard Kunstler, *The Geography of Nowhere* (New York: Simon and Schuster, 1993), pp. 76–78.

page 184: "the architect . . . used orange plastic webbing . . .": Belinda Luscombe, "Making a Splash," *Time,* 8 April 1996, p. 64.

page 184: "Instead of concentrating people in apartment blocks . . .": Witold Rybczynski, *City Life* (New York: Scribner, 1995), p. 229.

page 184: "an embarrassing foible of an aging master": Ibid.

page 188: "The present arrangement has certainly done away with sacred places . . .": James Howard Kunstler, *The Geography of Nowhere* (New York: Simon and Schuster, 1993), p. 119.

page 188: "The future of retailing in America may all come down to . . .": Bruce Horovitz, "Malls Are Like, Totally Uncool, Say Hip Teens," *USA Today,* 1 May 1996.

page 188: "All told in America, shopping mall vacancies . . .": Alan Ehrenhart, "Return to Main Street," *Governing,* May 1996, p. 25.

page 189: "abandon the fading strip mall . . .": Ibid., p. 26.

page 189: Commuters spend up to five hours a day . . .: Sonia Nazario, "Suburban Dreams Hit Roadblock," *Los Angeles Times,* 23 June 1996, Home edition.

page 190: "Neighborhoods Reborn: After a Half-Century Hiatus . . .": See "Neighborhoods Reborn," *Consumer Reports,* May 1996, pp. 24–30.

page 190: "restore existing urban centers and towns . . .": Congress for New Urbanism, Charter of the New Urbanism, p. 1.

page 191: "the only organized nationwide movement of consequence . . .": Herbert Muschamp, "Can New Urbanism Find Room for the Old?" *New York Times,* 2 June 1996.

page 191: "What are the key precepts of the new traditionalist community? . . .": Philip Langdon, "The New, Neighborly Architecture," *The American Enterprise,* November/December 1996, p. 42.

page 192: A sidewalk gives you the permission . . .: Karl Zinsmeister, "Coming Home to Community Life," *The American Enterprise,* November/December 1996, p. 4.

page 194: discussing the newest element to be added to Disneyworld . . .: Witold Rybczynski, "Tomorrowland," *The New Yorker,* 22 July 1996, pp. 36–39.

page 194: You would look in vain for manifestations . . .: Ibid., p. 37.

Chapter Eleven

page 201: "the city, far from being a cause of poverty . . .": Edward C. Banfield, *The Unheavenly City* (Boston and Toronto: Little, Brown and Company, 1970), p. 114.

page 202: "physical location, access to regional clusters . . .": Michael E. Porter, "The Competitive Advantage of the Inner City," *Harvard Business Review,* May/June 1995, pp. 57–62.

Select Bibliography

Abbott, Carl. *Portland: Planning, Politics, and Growth in a 20th Century City.* Lincoln: University of Nebraska Press, 1983.

Anderson, Harry H., and Frederic I. Olson. *Milwaukee: At the Gathering of the Waters.* Tulsa, Okla.: Continental Heritage Press, 1991.

Banfield, Edward C. *The Unheavenly City.* Boston and Toronto: Little, Brown and Company, 1970.

Barnes, Henry A. *The Man with the Red and Green Eyes.* New York: E.P. Dutton and Company, 1965.

Barnett, Jonathan. *The Fractured Metropolis.* New York: HarperCollins, IconEds, 1995.

Barone, Michael. "Government Gets a Shrink." *U.S. News and World Report,* 20 June 1994.

Beatty, Jack. *The Rascal King.* Reading, Mass.: Addison-Wesley, 1992.

Bel Geddes, Norman. *Magic Motorways.* New York: Random House, 1940.

Bernard, Richard M. *Snow Belt Cities.* Bloomington: Indiana University Press, 1990.

Bok, Derek. "Cities and Suburbs." In *Suburbs and Cities: Changing Patterns in Metropolitan Planning.* Washington, D.C.: The Aspen Institute, 1995.

Bovard, James. *The Fair Trade Fraud.* New York: St. Martin's Press, 1991.

———. "The U.S. Is Not the Victim of Unfair Trade Practices." In *Trade: Opposing Viewpoints,* edited by William Dudley. San Diego: Greenhaven Press, 1991.

Bulger, William. *While the Music Lasts.* New York: Houghton Mifflin Company, 1996.

221

Burns, Arthur E., and Edward A. Williams. *Federal Work, Security, and Relief Programs*. Research Monograph. Work Projects Administration, Division of Research. New York: DeCapo Press, 1971.

Cairncross, Frances. *Costing the Earth*. Boston: Harvard Business School Press, 1992.

Caro, Robert. *The Path to Power*. New York: Alfred A. Knopf, 1982.

———. *The Powerbroker*. New York: Alfred A. Knopf, 1974.

Chubb, John E., and Terry M. Moe. *Politics, Markets, and America's Schools*. Washington, D.C.: Brookings Institute, 1990.

"City vs. Country: Tom Peters and George Gilder Debate the Impact of Technology on Location." *Forbes ASAP*, 27 February 1995.

Congress for New Urbanism. "Charter of the New Urbanism."

Cookson, Peter, Jr. *School Choice: The Struggle for the Soul of American Education*. New Haven and London: Yale University Press, 1984.

Crowe, Sylvia. *The Landscape of Roads*. London: Architectural Press, 1960.

Dean, Andrea Oppenheimer. "Reflections from a Glass House." *Preservation*, July/August 1996.

Derus, Michele. "Central City Church Helps Immigrants Buy Homes." *Milwaukee Journal Sentinel*, 7 July 1996.

Dilulio, John J., Jr. "Prisons Are a Bargain, by Any Measure." *New York Times*, 16 January 1996.

Douglas, Paul. *America in the Marketplace*. New York: Holt, Rinehart and Winston, 1966.

Drucker, Peter. "Really Reinventing Government." *Atlantic*, February 1995.

Dugger, Celia W. "Immigrant Influence Rises in New York City in 1990s." *New York Times*, 9 January 1997.

Dunne, Nancy. *Financial Times*, 11 May 1993, London section.

"E for Effort Awards." *Financial World*, 1 February 1994.

Eggers, William D. *Rightsizing Government: Lessons from America's Public Sector Innovators*. Los Angeles: The Reason Foundation, 1994.

Eggers, William D., and John O'Leary. *Revolution at the Roots*. New York: The Free Press, 1995.

Ehrenhart, Alan. "Return to Main Street." *Governing*, May 1996.

El Nasser, Haya. "As Suburban Nests Empty, Couples Flocking to the City." *USA Today*, 4 November 1996.

Emshwiller, John R. "Empty Stores Still Dot the Riot-Torn Areas of L.A." *Wall Street Journal*, 22 May 1996.

Select Bibliography

Federal Highway Administration. "Man of the Century." *Public Roads,* special edition, 1996.

Financial World, News release. 23 February 1993.

Friedman, Milton. *Free to Choose.* San Diego: Harcourt Brace Jovanovich, 1991.

Fuerst, J. S. "Public Housing in the United States." In *Public Housing in Europe and America,* edited by J. S. Fuerst. New York: John Wiley and Sons, 1974.

Funiciello, Theresa. *Tyranny of Kindness.* New York: Atlantic Monthly Press, 1993.

Garreau, Joel. *Edge City: Life on the New Frontier.* New York: Doubleday, 1991.

Gelfand, Mark I. *A Nation of Cities.* New York and London: Oxford University Press, 1975.

Gilder, George F. *Life after Television.* Knoxville, Tenn.: Whittle Direct Books, 1990.

Glaeser, Edward L. "Why Economists Still Like Cities." *City Journal,* Spring 1996.

Glazer, Nathan. "City Leadership in Human Capital Investment." In *Interwoven Destinies,* edited by Henry G. Cisneros. New York: W. W. Norton and Co., 1993.

Gleck, Elizabeth. "The Impossible Dream." *Time,* 19 February 1996.

Glover, Charles. "The Challenge of a New Highway Program." In *Highway and the Landscape,* edited by W. Brewster Snow. New Brunswick, N.J.: Rutgers University Press, 1959.

Goode, W. Wilson. *In Goode Faith.* Valley Forge, Pa.: Judson Press, 1992.

Gordon, Fredrick. "Parole Stop Strengthens City's Attack on Crime." *Milwaukee Journal Sentinel,* 12 May 1996.

Gratz, Roberta Brandes. *The Living City.* New York: Simon and Schuster, 1989.

Greenberg, Reuben. *Let's Take Back Our Streets!* Chicago and New York: Contemporary Books, 1989.

Gurda, John. *The West End, Merrill Park, Pigsville, Concordia.* Milwaukee: Milwaukee Humanities Program, University of Wisconsin-Milwaukee, 1980.

Hagedorn, John M. *People and Folks.* Chicago: Lake View Press, 1988.

Hamill, Pete. *A Drinking Life: A Memoir.* Boston: Little, Brown, 1994.

Hanushek, Eric A. "Making America's Schools Work." *The Brooking Review,* Fall 1994.

Harmer, David. *School Choice*. Washington, D.C.: Cato Institute, 1994.

Hawken, Paul. *The Ecology of Commerce*. New York: HarperBusiness, 1993.

Hoan, Daniel. Inaugural address prepared texts, various. Milwaukee Public Library Archives.

Horovitz, Bruce. "Malls Are Like, Totally Uncool, Say Hip Teens." *USA Today*, 1 May 1996.

Huseck, Howard. "We Don't Need Subsidized Housing." *City Journal*, Winter 1997.

Ingraham, Joseph. "Politics and Road Building." In *Highway and the Landscape*, edited by W. Brewster Snow. New Brunswick, N.J.: Rutgers University Press, 1959.

Jacobs, Jane. *Cities and the Wealth of Nations*. New York: Random House, 1984.

———. *The Death and Life of Great American Cities*. New York: Random House, 1961.

Jones, Tim. "Detroit Sees a Glimmer of Renaissance." *Chicago Tribune*, 22 November 1996.

Kass, John. "Dinkins Calls for NY Meeting." *Chicago Tribune*, 20 June 1990.

Kelling, George L. "How to Run a Police Department." *City Journal*, Autumn 1995.

Kenny, Judith T., and Thomas C. Hubka. "City Reform versus Neighborhood Traditions: Milwaukee's Urban Reform Efforts and the Housing Goals of the Polish Community, 1900–1920." *Research and Opinion*. Milwaukee: Urban Research Center, University of Wisconsin-Milwaukee, April 1996.

Kerstein, Edward S. *Milwaukee's All-American Mayor*. Englewood, N.J.: Prentice-Hall, 1966.

Kinney, Ken. "Should Property Taxes Subsidize Automobile Usage?" City of Milwaukee Strategic Planning Staff Report, March 1991.

Kohr, Leopold. *The Inner City*. Talybont, Wales: Y Lolfa, 1989.

Kozol, Jonathan. *Savage Inequalities*. New York: Crown Publishers, 1991.

Kunstler, James Howard. *The Geography of Nowhere*. New York: Simon and Schuster, 1993.

———. "On the Road: It's Life on Long Island." *Newsday*, 16 June 1996.

Lambert, Bruce. "Suburban Nassau County Makes Plans to Turn a Sprawling Center into a Focal Hub." *New York Times*, 18 January 1997.

Select Bibliography

Landscape Research. *Built in Milwaukee: An Architectural Overview of the City.* A report prepared for the City of Milwaukee, 1991.

Langdon, Philip. "The New, Neighborly Architecture." *The American Enterprise,* November/December 1996.

Leys, Ron. "Obsolete Dam Is Monument to Lost Causes." *Milwaukee Journal,* 18 February 1990.

Low Income Housing Special Information Service. Special memorandum, 1993.

Lucas, Eric. "Lakeside Legacy." *Midwest Express Magazine,* May/June 1996.

Luscombe, Belinda. "Making a Splash." *Time,* 8 April 1996.

Maier, Henry W. Inaugural address prepared texts, various. Milwaukee Public Library Archives.

———. Mayor's Transportation Message, draft no. 5 prepared text. Milwaukee Public Library Archives.

Makower, Joel. *The E-Factor.* New York: Tilden Press, 1993.

McFarland, M. Carter. *Federal Government and Urban Problems.* Boulder, Colo.: Westview Press, 1978.

McGroarty, Daniel. *Break These Chains: The Battle for School Choice.* Rocklin, Calif.: Forum, 1996.

Mead, Lawrence. "Growing a Smaller Welfare State." *New York Times,* 3 December 1995.

Milwaukee Drug Abatement Project. "Statistical Report: Numbers for entire program thru 8/6/96."

Mittford, Jessica. *The American Way of Death.* New York: Simon and Schuster, 1963.

Moynihan, Daniel Patrick. "ISTEA's Principal Author, Senator Moynihan, Shares Views." *U.S. Mayor,* 23 December 1996.

Mullins, Robert. "Cracking Walnut Street's Woes." *The Business Journal,* 29 April 1995.

Mumford, Lewis. *The City in History.* New York: Harcourt Brace, 1961.

———. *The Highway and the City.* New York: Harcourt Brace Jovanovich, 1963.

Murray, Charles. *Losing Ground: American Social Policy, 1950–1980.* New York: Basic Books, 1984.

Muschamp, Herbert. "Can New Urbanism Find Room for the Old?" *New York Times,* 2 June 1996.

Mydans, Seth. "Gangs Go Public in New Fight for Respect." *New York Times,* 2 May 1993.

Naisbitt, John, and Patricia Aburdene. *Megatrends 2000.* New York: Morrow, 1990.

"Neighborhoods Reborn." *Consumer Reports,* May 1996.

The New Hope Project. "Progress Report," June 1996.

1993 World Almanac. New York: Pharos Books, 1992.

Olasky, Marvin. *The Tragedy of American Compassion.* Washington, D.C.: Regnery Gateway, 1992.

Ortega, Bob. "Portland Shows Nation's Planners How to Guide Growth." *Wall Street Journal,* 26 December 1995.

Ottman, Jacquelyn. *Green Marketing.* Lincolnwood, Ill.: NTC Business Books, 1990.

Pacelle, Mitchell. "Some Urban Planners Say Downtowns Need a Lot More Congestion." *New York Times,* 7 August 1996.

Peirce, Neal R. *Citistates.* Washington, D.C.: Seven Locks Press, 1993.

Peters, Thomas J. *In Search of Excellence: Lessons from America's Best Companies.* New York: Harper and Row, 1982.

Peterson, William. "Free Trade Is the Best Trading System." In *Trade: Opposing Viewpoints,* edited by William Dudley. San Diego: Greenhaven Press, 1991.

Porter, Michael E. "The Competitive Advantage of the Inner City." *Harvard Business Review,* May/June 1995.

Powell, John A. "Tax Policy and Racial Segregation in Housing." American Bar Association Tax and Social Policy Forum, 2 August 1996.

"Prague Transformed." *The Economist,* 18 November 1995.

Quartel, Robert. "The Jones Act: Keep It or Kill It?" *The Journal of Commerce,* 11 July 1996.

Rendell, Ed. "Privatization 1996." Remarks to the Reason Foundation conference, Los Angeles, September 1995.

Riemer, David R. *The Prisoners of Welfare.* New York: Praeger, 1988.

———. "Replacing Welfare with Work: The Case for an Employment Maintenance Model." *Focus,* Winter 1994/95 (University of Wisconsin-Madison Institute for Research on Poverty).

Roberts, Paul. "The Durning Point." *Utne Reader,* August 1996.

Rusk, David. *Cities without Suburbs.* Washington, D.C.: The Woodrow Wilson Center Press, 1993.

Select Bibliography

Rybczynski, Witold. *City Life.* New York: Scribner, 1995.

——. "Tomorrowland." *The New Yorker,* 22 July 1996.

Schlenker, Thomas, and Kathleen Fessler. "Measles in Milwaukee." *Wisconsin Medical Journal,* July 1990.

Schneider, Kenneth. *On the Nature of Cities.* San Francisco: Jossey-Bass Publishers, 1979.

Sclar, Elliot D., and Walter Hook. "The Importance of Cities to the National Economy." In *Interwoven Destinies,* edited by Henry G. Cisneros. New York: W. W. Norton and Company, 1993.

Sherwood, Robert. *Roosevelt and Hopkins.* New York: Harper and Brothers, 1948.

Snow, W. Brewster, and W. A. Bugge. "The Complete Highway." In *Highway and the Landscape,* edited by W. Brewster Snow. New Brunswick, N.J.: Rutgers University Press, 1959.

Soucie, Kevin. "The End of the Road." *Isthmus,* 29 September 1995.

——. "Lane Change." *Milwaukee Journal,* 15 January 1995.

Sundquist, James. *Dispersing Population.* Washington, D.C.: Brookings Institute, 1975.

Task Force on Federal Policy and Family Poverty. "Report to the National League of Cities Board of Directors." July 1993.

Thurow, Lester. *The Zero Sum Society.* New York: Basic Books, 1980.

U.S. Bureau of the Census. *1993 American Housing Survey.* Washington, D.C.

Welfeld, Irving. *HUD Scandals.* New Brunswick, N.J.: Transaction Publishers, 1992.

Wells, Robert W. *This Is Milwaukee.* Garden City, N.J.: Doubleday, 1970.

——. *Yesterday's Milwaukee.* Miami: E. A. Seaman, 1976.

Weyrich, Paul, and William S. Lind. *Conservatives and Mass Transit: Is It Time for a New Look?* Washington, D.C.: Free Congress Foundation, 1996.

Wills, Garry. *Lincoln at Gettysburg.* New York: Simon and Schuster, 1992.

Wines, Michael. *New York Times,* 24 September 1995.

Wolfe, Tom. *From Bauhaus to Our House.* New York: Farrar, Straus and Giroux, 1981.

Zinsmeister, Karl. "Coming Home to Community Life." *The American Enterprise,* November/December 1996.

Index

Index

Index

Index

Index

Williams, Kitty, 7
Williams, Polly, 87–88
Wills, Garry, 106
Wilson, James Q., 59
Wines, Michael, 69
Wolfe, Thomas, 183
Works Progress Administration
(WPA), 72
World War II, 72

post-, 11–12, 73, 201
Wright, Frank Lloyd, 184, 185

Youth Diversion Project, 52

Zero Sum Society, The, 143
Zinsmeister, Karl, 192
Zoning, 105–108, 121, 147–149